The END TIMES
IN CHRONOLOGICAL
ORDER
WORKBOOK

RON RHODES

HARVEST PROPHECY
AN IMPRINT OF HARVEST HOUSE PUBLISHERS

Cover design by the Dugan Design Group

Cover photo © by sdecoret / Adobe Stock

Timeline illustration by Terry Dugan, Dugan Design Group

Interior design by Rockwell Davis

For bulk, special sales, or ministry purchases, please call 1-800-547-8979. Email: Customerservice@hhpbooks.com

The End Times in Chronological Order Workbook

Copyright © 2022 by Ron Rhodes
Published by Harvest House Publishers
Eugene, Oregon 97408
www.harvesthousepublishers.com

ISBN 978-0-7369-8538-3 (pbk)
ISBN 978-0-7369-8539-0 (eBook)

Printed in the United States of America

22 23 24 25 26 27 28 29 / CM / 10 9 8 7 6 5 4 3 2 1

For Carter and Bennett

Acknowledgments

Few books are solo efforts. As any author will tell you, most books involve a lot of work not only by the author but also by countless other individuals. A book is shaped by the author's personal interactions with his family, friends, and professional colleagues, as well as by folks at church, readers, conference attendees, radio listeners who send emails, and—especially—the many members of the publishing team. The more books I write, the more I sense my indebtedness to numerous individuals in all these areas and more.

While I desire to thank everyone I can think of, space limitations allow me to single out only a few. I remain forever thankful for my family—my wife, Kerri, my two grown children, David and Kylie, and my two grandsons, Carter and Bennett. Continued heartfelt appreciation goes to the entire staff at Harvest House Publishers—especially Bob Hawkins and Steve Miller. I also want to single out my editor, Rod Morris, and interior designer, Rockwell Davis, who created the layout for this workbook. Most of all, I express profound thanks and appreciation to our Lord Jesus Christ, who Himself is the heart and center of biblical prophecy. May He be glorified in this workbook!

CONTENTS

Introducing
Biblical Prophecy

Today we are witnessing:

- a massive falling away from the truth

- a widespread embracing of doctrinal error

- a profound moral decline

- a growing tolerance for all things evil

- a widespread outbreak of a variety of sexual sins and perversions, with no repentance in sight

- the steady diminishing of religious freedom

- the ever-increasing global persecution of God's people

- Israel being a relentless sore spot in the world

- ever-escalating conflict in the Middle East

- efforts being made toward rebuilding the Jewish temple

- the stage being set for a massive invasion of Israel by Russia and Muslim nations

- the steady rise and influence of globalism

- political and economic steps toward the establishment of a revived Roman Empire—*a United States of Europe*

- the emergence of a cashless world in preparation for the antichrist's control of the world economy during the tribulation

- and much more.

Does it seem to you that world circumstances are growing more troubling with each passing decade? Give some examples. *Political Control through Covid Banks etc.*

What are the most pressing initial questions you have about Bible prophecy?

It is sobering—*sometimes frightening*—to witness all that is transpiring in our present day. Current events are setting the stage for the future tribulation period. It therefore makes great sense to go through a workbook strategically designed to guide you in understanding the prophetic Scriptures.

How do you think an understanding of Bible prophecy might help us keep current events—*even horrible events*—in proper perspective?

This workbook is a stand-alone guide to understanding biblical prophecy. It does not require that you have previously read my book *The End Times in Chronological Order*. The workbook will make perfect sense to you all by itself.

For those who have read my previous book, this workbook will also benefit you. It not only reviews essential truths but also guides you step-by-step through the Scriptures. Trust me—there is great blessing in sifting prophetic truths directly from the pages of Scripture.

It is my hope and prayer that as you study this workbook, you will grow firm in the following convictions:

- The Bible is the Word of God.

- God knows the future.

- God is in sovereign control of all that occurs in the world.

- God has a plan for humanity—*and a plan for you*.

- God will one day providentially cause good to triumph over evil.

- A new world is coming—*a "new earth."*

- We'll all receive body upgrades—*glorified resurrection bodies*.

- The Lord is coming *soon*!

I can promise you that a study of Bible prophecy will change your life. It certainly has mine. My exposure to biblical prophecy was a vital contributing factor to my becoming a Christian back in the 1970s. (*Wow, have I been around that long?*)

Now, here is an important foundational point: *Prophecy is God's specific revelation regarding future events.* The backdrop is that only God—who is omniscient (or all-knowing)—knows the future. In Isaiah 46:9-11, God Himself affirms:

> "I am God, and there is no other;
>> I am God, and there is none like me,
> declaring the end from the beginning
>> and from ancient times things not yet done,
> saying, 'My counsel shall stand,
> and I will accomplish all my purpose.'"

This means that our sovereign God controls human history. He is also the only one who can reveal the future to us. And He does so in the pages of the Bible.

I find it fascinating that about 25 percent of divine revelation in the Bible was prophetic when originally written. This means that one out of every four verses in the Bible is prophetic. Such prophetic verses typically deal with Jesus Christ, Israel, the church, the Gentiles, Satan, the antichrist, the signs of the times, the various end-time judgments, Armageddon, the second coming, the millennial kingdom, and the eternal state.

Why is it significant that one-fourth of the Bible is prophetic? Be specific.

In this workbook, I will serve as your tour guide through the pages of prophetic Scripture. By the time we're done, you will have a thorough understanding of biblical prophecy.

Each lesson has the following helpful features:

Key Concept: This is a concise statement of the primary focus of the lesson.

The Big Ideas in This Lesson: These bullet points give you the big picture.

Probing the Scriptures: I examine key Bible verses relevant to the lesson. Questions will be sprinkled throughout.

Life Lessons: These are applicational life-changing truths based upon Scripture.

Digging Deeper with Cross-References: These cross-references provide extra clarity on crucial biblical concepts.

Prayer: We close each lesson by talking to God about what we've learned.

My personal prayer is that this workbook will cause a significant change in the way you view this present world and your place in it. Scripture itself says prophecy ought to have a life-changing effect on us (see, for example, Titus 2:11-14). So this workbook ultimately seeks to make a difference in the way you live your Christian life.

I know there are some who say the prophetic future makes them fearful. Bible prophecy, properly understood, should have the opposite effect. It should make believers confident and bold as they trust in the God who controls the prophetic future.

> What truths can you sift from the following verses about why we should not be fearful in the end times?
>
> - John 14:1— *Let not your ♡ be troubled! I Go to prepare a place for you. I will come recieve you to my self*
>
> - John 14:27— *Peace I give & leave with you.*
>
> - John 16:33— *In Jesus we may have peace he has overcome the world*
>
> - Matthew 6:34— *Dont worry about tommorrow*

There's one more thing. Seven times in the book of Revelation we are told that those who study and obey the truths in the book will receive a special blessing. I *want* that blessing, don't you?

> Briefly scan through Revelation 1:3, 14:13, 16:15, 19:9, 20:6, and 22:7, 14. How are these verses motivational? *Blessed are those who follow after Jesus.*
> *"Blessed"*
>
> Since seven is a number representing *perfection* and *completeness*, what is the significance of seven pronouncements of blessing for those who read and obey the book of Revelation?
>
> *They may have the right to the tree of life & enter through the gate*

It might interest you to know that, as a general principle, Scripture consistently teaches that obedience to God's Word brings you good things in life. Obedience to God yields:

- blessing (Revelation 1:3; Luke 11:28)

- long life (1 Kings 3:14; John 8:51)

- happiness (Psalm 112:1; 119:56)

- peace (Proverbs 1:33)

- well-being (Jeremiah 7:23)

That's a pretty impressive list. Obeying God is not always easy. But I'm willing to work hard in learning obedience since those blessings are hard to pass up!

Let me encourage you that as you learn prophetic truths from this workbook, allow what you learn to become a part of the fabric of your life. As your mind feasts on these truths, let your heart also be enriched, nurtured, and changed for the better. Seek to follow and obey. *You will be blessed!*

> *Lord, by the power of Your Spirit, please enable me to understand and apply the truths we examine from prophetic Scripture. Please inspire and excite me with Your Word. Instill in me a sense of awe for the Lord Jesus Christ, who Himself is the heart and center of Bible prophecy. Thank You in Jesus's name. Amen.*

Blessed = Divine Favor

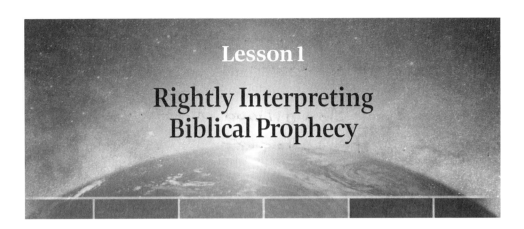

Lesson 1
Rightly Interpreting Biblical Prophecy

◼ KEY CONCEPT

God is the ultimate Author of prophecy, and He wants you to understand it.

◼ THE BIG IDEAS IN THIS LESSON

- We can trust the prophecies in the Bible because they come from God.

- Old Testament prophecies of Christ's first coming were all fulfilled literally. This sets a precedent. Prophecies of the second coming will be fulfilled just as literally.

- Simple interpretive rules guide us in rightly understanding Bible prophecy.

◼ PROBING THE SCRIPTURES

You Can Trust Prophetic Scripture

God has the unmatched ability to predict the future with 100 percent accuracy.

Briefly summarize God's claims in the following verses:

- Isaiah 44:7-8— *Who Can proclaim as God. He appointed things that came + is 2 come. els there a God Beside me!*

- Isaiah 45:21— *A just God & Saviour there is none beside me!* *notone*

- Isaiah 46:8-10— *For I am God none beside me none like me*

- Isaiah 48:3, 5— *God declared it from the beginning & it came to pass*

Our all-knowing God provides everything He wants us to know about Him, and how we can have a relationship with Him, in the pages of Scripture. He is the one who caused the Bible to be written. Through it, He speaks to us today just as He spoke to people in ancient times when its words were first given.

The Bible is not man-made. It is *God-inspired*. The original documents of the Bible were written by men who were permitted to exercise their own personalities and literary talents—but *they wrote under the control and guidance of the Holy Spirit.*

What evidence do you see about how God's Spirit spoke through the human authors of Scripture in the following verses?

- Zechariah 7:12—

- 2 Samuel 23:2— *His word was on my tongue*

- 2 Timothy 3:16-17— *All scrip. is given by Inspiration*

- 2 Peter 1:21— *Holy men of God spoke as they were moved by the Holy Spirit*

Word Study: The Greek word translated "carried along" in 2 Peter 1:21 literally means "forcefully borne along." Even though human beings were used in writing down God's prophecies, these men were all sovereignly *borne along* by the Holy Spirit. The human wills of the authors were not the originators of God's message.

How did Jesus Himself confirm the divine authority of Scripture in the following verses?

- Matthew 4:4— *Man shall not live by bread alone but by every word from God's mouth*

- Matthew 5:17-18— *He came to fulfill the law*

- Matthew 15:1-6—

- John 17:17— *Your word is truth*

Based on these verses, formulate a one-sentence summary of Jesus's view of Scripture.

Truth already written by God to be fulfilled

A Literal Approach Is Best

A literal approach to interpreting prophecy is best. This approach embraces the normal, everyday, common understanding of the words found in Scripture. We see this illustrated in prophecies of Christ's first coming:

What does a literal understanding of Micah 5:2 indicate about Jesus's birth city?

Out of you though little shall come the Ruler in Israel

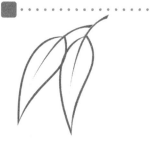

What does a literal understanding of Isaiah 7:14 indicate about the miraculous nature of Jesus's birth? *The virgin birth shall conceive & Bear a Son*

What does a literal understanding of Zechariah 12:10 indicate about the nature of Jesus's death? *A spirit of favor & supplication*

Just as a literal understanding of the prophecies of Christ's first coming makes great sense, so a literal understanding of the prophecies of Christ's second coming makes great sense.

What do you learn about the second coming based on a literal understanding of the following verses?

- Matthew 16:27— *Son of man shall come w/ his angels in the glory of his father*

- Luke 12:40— *Son of man comes unexpectedly*

- Philippians 3:20— *We await Jesus from heaven*

Exceptions to a Literal Approach

There are some exceptions to a strictly literal approach. After all, not *every* statement in the Bible is intended to be taken literally. Let's briefly consider how these nonliteral statements in Scripture can be understood.

The Literal Method Does Not Eliminate Figures of Speech

The Bible contains some figures of speech. But these figures of speech always teach us something literal.

To illustrate, try to sift out some literal truths from the figures of speech about God or Jesus in the following verses:

- God's "wings" in Psalm 91:4— *Resting in him*
  His faithfulness is our shield

- God as a "rock" in Psalm 94:22—
  His our defence

- Jesus as a "vine" in John 15:4-5— *Believing Jesus is Gods*
  Son Staying faithful in him.

In each case, these figures of speech teach us something literal about God or Jesus.

The Literal Method Does Not Eliminate the Use of Symbols

While the Bible often makes use of symbols, each symbol conveys something literal. In the book of Revelation, the symbols are often defined for us in the immediate context:

Read Revelation 1:20. What are the "seven stars" that are in Christ's right hand? What are the "seven golden lampstands"?

Angels of the 7 Churches

Read Revelation 5:8. What are the "golden bowls full of incense"?

prayer of Saints

> Read Revelation 17:15. How are "the waters" defined?
>
> *people, multitudes, nations & tongues*

Textual clues often point us to the literal truth found in a symbol, either in the immediate context or in the broader context of the whole of Scripture.

The Literal Method Does Not Eliminate the Use of Parables

Jesus often used parables that are not to be taken literally. Yet—like symbols—each parable conveys a literal point. To illustrate, following are a few of Jesus's parables, with a concise summary of their meaning:

The Parable of the Wheat and Weeds (Matthew 13:24-30) reveals that true and false believers will coexist and be mingled together until the future judgment when they will be separated.

The Parable of the Mustard Seed (Matthew 13:31-32) reveals that the kingdom started small, but it will grow immeasurably large.

The Parable of the Fishing Net (Matthew 13:47-50) reveals that up until Christ's second coming, when judgment will take place, there will be both genuine Christians and phony (professing) Christians that coexist within the kingdom.

The Parable of the Fig Tree (Luke 21:29-31) reveals that as prophetic "signs of the times" come to pass, Christ's followers will recognize them and be prepared for the Lord's coming.

The Parable of the Faithful Servant (Matthew 24:45-51) reveals that those who profess to serve Christ during the future tribulation period must make a pivotal choice—be faithful and obedient servants or be unfaithful and disobedient servants.

The Parables of the Talents (Matthew 25:14-30) reveals that the more faithful we are in serving God in the present life, the more we will be entrusted with in the next life.

Biblical Confirmation of Literalness

Though there are some figures of speech, symbols, and parables in the Bible, the biblical text itself provides numerous confirmations of the *overall literalness* of the biblical text. You can check this out for yourself:

> How does Exodus 20:11 confirm the earlier Genesis account of creation?
>
> *In 6 days the Lord made heaven & earth*

> How does 1 Timothy 2:13 confirm the Genesis account of Adam and Eve's creation?
>
> *For Adam was formed 1st then Eve*
>
> How does Romans 5:12 confirm the Genesis account of Adam's fall into sin?
>
> *As sin came in through 1 man*
>
> How does Matthew 24:37-39 confirm the truth of Noah's flood?
>
> *As were the days of noah so will be the coming of the son of man*
>
> How does Matthew 12:38-41 confirm the account of Jonah and the big fish?
>
> *For as Jonah was 3 days & 3 nights in the fish so will the son of man be in the gloh earth*

We might say that the literal method of interpretation is built into the very fabric of Scripture itself.

You Can Understand Prophetic Scripture

Here is a promise you can count on: *You can understand prophetic Scripture.*

To accomplish this, it is essential to follow some basic rules of interpretation. It is the rule-based interpreter who "correctly explains the word of truth" (2 Timothy 2:15 NLT). Following are some simple rules to remember:

1. Always Seek the Plain Sense

Drill this principle into your mind: *When the plain sense makes good sense, seek no other sense lest you end up in nonsense.* This is the foundational principle that has always guided me in interpreting Bible prophecy. It will guide you as well.

2. Submit All Doctrinal Presuppositions to Scripture

All interpreters are influenced to some degree by personal, theological, and denominational prejudices. None of us approaches Scripture with a blank slate. For this reason, our doctrinal opinions must be in harmony with Scripture and *subject to correction by it.* We must allow the biblical text itself to modify or reshape our presuppositions and beliefs.

3. Pay Close Attention to the Context

Every word in the Bible is part of a sentence, every sentence is part of a paragraph, every paragraph is part of a book, and every book is part of the whole of Scripture. The interpretation of a specific passage must not contradict the broader teaching of Scripture on a point.

4. Make a Correct Genre Judgment

The Bible contains various literary genres, each of which has particular characteristics that we must recognize to interpret the text correctly. Biblical genres include history (Acts), the dramatic epic (Job), poetry (Psalms), wise sayings (Proverbs), and apocalyptic writings (Daniel and Revelation). Incorrect genre judgments will lead us astray when interpreting Scripture.

For example:

- Poetry (such as a psalm that contains symbols) should not be treated as a straightforward narrative.

- A parable should not be treated as history.

Even though the Bible contains various literary genres, some of which include symbols, the biblical authors most often used literal statements to convey their ideas. *Where the Bible writers use a literal means to express their ideas, the Bible student must use a literal approach in interpreting such ideas.*

5. Consult History and Culture

The Bible student should try to step out of his or her Western mindset and into an ancient Jewish mindset. It is wise to consider Jewish marriage rites, burial rites, family practices, farm practices, business practices, the monetary system, methods of warfare, slavery, the treatment of captives, the use of covenants, and religious practices. Armed with such detailed historical information, interpreting the Bible becomes much easier.

6. Remember That One Prophetic Passage May Apply to More Than One Event

A prophecy in the Bible may refer to two events that are separated by a significant period. Though found in a single passage, these events are blended into one picture, masking the intervening period. The time gap is not recognized within the particular text, but it becomes evident in consultation with other verses.

An example is Zechariah 9:9-10. This passage prophesies both the first and second comings of Jesus Christ:

What do we learn about Jesus at His first coming in Zechariah 9:9?

His humble riding on a donkey

What do we learn about Jesus at His second coming and His millennial kingdom in Zechariah 9:10?

His dominion will be from 1 sea to another
From Great River to Ends of the Earth

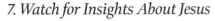

7. Watch for Insights About Jesus

From beginning to end—from Genesis to Revelation—the Bible is a Jesus book. Prophetic Scripture consistently points to Him!

What did Jesus say to some Jews about how Scripture points to Him (John 5:39-40)? *These are they that bear witness of me   Jesus*

How did Jesus help the two disciples on the road to Emmaus see that Scripture points to Him (Luke 24:25-27)?

He explained to them things concerning himself in all Scripture

What did Jesus say to His disciples about how Scripture points to Him (Luke 24:44)? *These all the things I spoke while I was w/ you that all things must be fulfilled which were written*

The interpreter of Bible prophecy is wise to look for Jesus in the biblical text! Our interpretation of prophetic Scripture ought to be *Christocentric* (centered on Christ).

What evidence do you see in Revelation 1 that Revelation is a Christ-centered book? Be specific. *The Rev. of Jesus Christ*

What implications does the Christ-centered nature of Scripture have for your own life being Christ-centered?

Jesus and Bible Prophecy	
Jesus is building the New Jerusalem	John 14:1-3; Revelation 21
Jesus will come for us at the rapture	1 Thessalonians 4:13-17
Jesus will judge Christians in heaven	2 Corinthians 5:10
Jesus will inflict judgments during the tribulation period	Revelation 6
Jesus will come again (the "second coming")	Revelation 19:11-21
Jesus will judge the nations after the second coming	Matthew 25:31-46
Jesus will reign during the millennial kingdom	Revelation 20:1-5
Jesus will judge the wicked dead after the millennium	Revelation 20:11-15

LIFE LESSONS

Bible prophecy has a practical side to it. We can learn essential truths from prophecy that help us to be better Christians. Here are a few life lessons to keep in mind:

Prophecy Proves the Bible Is God's Word

1. God alone knows the prophetic future.
2. God shares multiple specific prophecies of the future in the pages of the Bible and *no other holy book*.
3. Over 100 Old Testament messianic prophecies of Christ's first coming confirm God's 100-percent accuracy rate in foretelling the future.
4. Prophecy is thus a compelling proof that the Bible is God's Word and can be trusted.

Never doubt the Bible.

God Has an Eternal Purpose

1. Human history, in all its details, is but the outworking of the eternal purposes of God.

2. What has happened in the past, what is happening today, and what will happen in the prophetic future is all evidence of the unfolding of a purposeful plan devised by the personal God of the Bible (Ephesians 3:11; 2 Timothy 1:9).

3. *You* are part of God's eternal purpose. Never forget it.

DIGGING DEEPER WITH CROSS-REFERENCES

Prophecy

- Prophecy does not derive from human beings—2 Peter 1:21.
- God's prophetic word is certain—Ezekiel 12:26-28.
- God knows the end from the beginning—Isaiah 46:8-11.
- God fulfills the prophet's message—Isaiah 44:26.
- Prophecy involves a sure word from God—2 Peter 1:19.

We Can Trust Our All-Knowing God

- There is blessing in trusting God—Psalm 40:4.
- Trust God—He will help you—Psalm 37:5.
- Trust God in times of trouble—Psalm 50:14-15.
- Trust God at all times—Psalm 62:8.
- Trust in the Lord, not human beings—Psalm 118:8.
- Trust God with your whole heart—Proverbs 3:5-6.

PRAYER

Lord, please open my eyes and enhance my understanding so I can grasp all that You want me to learn in this workbook about Bible prophecy. By Your Spirit, I also ask You to enable me to apply the truths I learn to my daily life and be guided each moment by Your Word. Thank You in Jesus's name. Amen.

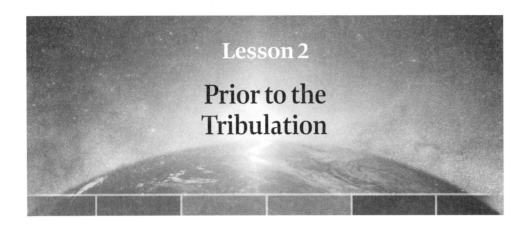

Lesson 2

Prior to the Tribulation

KEY CONCEPT

Biblical prophecy addresses not just the rapture and the tribulation period and beyond, but also the current age.

THE BIG IDEAS IN THIS LESSON

- God has a sovereign purpose for both Israel and the church during the current age.

- A super-sign of the end times is the birth of the modern, self-governing nation of Israel in 1948.

- Apostasy will escalate dramatically in the end times.

- The United States will apparently weaken in the end times. The balance of power will eventually shift toward a United States of Europe—a revived Roman Empire.

PROBING THE SCRIPTURES

A Divine Purpose for the Current Age

Biblical prophecy addresses not only end-time events such as the rapture, the tribulation period, the second coming of Christ, the millennial kingdom, and the eternal state, but also the current age in which we live. Foundationally, biblical prophecy reveals that God has a distinct divine purpose for both Israel and the church in the current age.

God's Purpose for Israel

Jesus did not fit the first-century Jews' preconceived ideas about the Messiah (Matthew 12:14, 24). They thought He'd be a political and military leader who would deliver them from Roman bondage. Jesus didn't do that, and the Jews ended up flatly rejecting Him as the promised Messiah.

What are some modern misconceptions of Jesus and His mission?

How can we avoid misconceptions of Jesus? Be specific.

Because of the Jewish rejection of Jesus, God inflicted upon them a partial judicial blindness and hardness as a judgment. Israel lost its favored position before God. The gospel was then preached to the Gentiles to make the Jews jealous so that they may yet be saved (Romans 11:11). We will see that in the end, God's people will include both Jews *and* Gentiles.

Read about God's covenant with Abraham in Genesis 12:1-3. How does verse 3 indicate that God ultimately wanted both Jews and Gentiles to be blessed through salvation in Jesus (who was a descendent of Abraham)?

Here are two things not to miss:

1. Since the time of the Jewish rejection of Christ, Gentiles who place faith in Jesus become members of God's church.
2. Jews who believe in Jesus also become members of God's church in the current age (see Ephesians 3:1-10; Colossians 1:24-29).

The best is yet to come: Israel's judicial blindness and hardness are only temporary. Toward the end of the tribulation period, the Jews will be in dire threat from the forces of the antichrist at Armageddon. At that time, God will remove Israel's blindness, and the Jewish remnant will finally recognize that Jesus is indeed the Messiah. They will

promptly turn to Him for rescue from the invading forces of the antichrist (Zechariah 12:10; see also Romans 11:13-14). *A remnant of Israel will thus be saved!*

Read Romans 11:25-27. Summarize how the apostle Paul speaks of Israel's future salvation.

God's Purpose for the Church

Acts 17:26 tells us that from one man, Adam, God "has made every nationality to live over the whole earth and has determined their appointed times and the boundaries of where they live" (CSB). God sovereignly chose *where* we'd live and *when* we'd live.

Today, you and I are living in the church age. The universal church is the ever-enlarging body of born-again believers who comprise the body of Christ and over whom He reigns as Lord (Galatians 3:28; Ephesians 4:1-6). This body comprises *only* believers in Christ. The way one becomes a member of this universal body is to simply place faith in Christ (Acts 16:31; Ephesians 2:8-9). If you're a believer, *you're in*!

Scripture instructs that each of us ought to be about the business of "rightly dividing the word of truth" (2 Timothy 2:15 KJV). Among other things, this means we must distinguish (*rightly divide*) between Israel and the church.

The church has not always existed. Seven fast facts confirm this conclusion:

1. The Old Testament does not contain a single reference to "the church."

2. Jesus said: "I *will* build my church" (Matthew 16:18). Notice the future tense. At the time Jesus spoke these words, the church did not yet exist.

3. The apostle Paul, the author of 1 Corinthians, wrote about the church and Israel as distinct from each other (1 Corinthians 10:32).

4. Every believer in the church age is baptized into the body of Christ (1 Corinthians 12:13), which first happened on the day of Pentecost (Acts 2; 11:15-16).

5. The church is called a "mystery" that was not revealed to past generations but was revealed for the first time in the New Testament era (Ephesians 3:3-6, 9; Colossians 1:26-27).

6. The church is built on the foundation of Christ's resurrection (Ephesians 1:19-20), meaning it could not have existed in Old Testament times.

7. The church is called a "new man" in Ephesians 2:15.

From a prophetic standpoint, why do you think it is essential to keep God's purposes for Israel and the church distinct?

What interpretive problems might arise if we confuse the two?

If you run into trouble answering these questions, here is an additional question that might put you on the right track:

Which of the two following scenarios represents your viewpoint?

- God is a promise-keeper who will fulfill *all* His promises to Israel from Old Testament times, including His promise to give Israel a permanent land in a future kingdom—the millennial kingdom (Genesis 15:18-21; 26:3-4; 28:13-14; Psalm 105:8-11).

- God will *not* literally fulfill His promises to Israel. Instead, He will spiritually fulfill them somehow in the church.

Spoiler Alert: I believe God is a promise-keeper and that He will give Israel precisely what He promised Israel. He'll also give the church exactly what He's promised the church.

What do the following verses reveal about God being a promise-keeper?

- Numbers 23:19—

- Deuteronomy 7:9—

- Joshua 21:45—

- Joshua 23:14—

- 1 Kings 8:56—

My friends, I believe God is truly faithful. He will fulfill *all* of His promises. These promises are foundational to the prophetic future.

The Course of the Present Age

Prophetic Scripture describes what the world will be like between Christ's first and second comings. Foundationally, because the Jews rejected Christ (and His kingdom offer) in the first century, God's kingdom program was thereby altered—*its establishment was delayed*. It will be postponed until after the second coming of Christ when Christ Himself will establish His thousand-year millennial kingdom.

In Matthew 13, Jesus revealed what the course of the present age will be like up until His second coming. Many of Jesus's prophetic statements relate to the growth of the church. For example, during the present age people will have varied responses to the gospel. These varied responses are rooted in the various forces that oppose the gospel—the world, the flesh, and the devil (Matthew 13:1-33). Some people will respond favorably, many others not.

Moreover, a false counter-sowing will imitate the true sowing of the gospel seed during this time. Only a judgment following the future tribulation period will separate true believers from unbelievers or false believers (Matthew 13:24-30, 36-43). Meanwhile, our gracious and patient God is providing plenty of time for people to turn to Him for salvation.

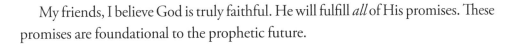

Have you ever wondered why the second coming of Christ has not already occurred? Have you ever wondered why God doesn't bring about the end immediately? Explain.

Read 2 Peter 3:8-10. Summarize what you learn.

Another key component of the current age relates specifically to Israel. The birth of the modern, self-governing nation of Israel in 1948 began the fulfillment of specific Bible prophecies about an international regathering of the Jews *in unbelief* before the judgments to come during the future tribulation period. This regathering was predicted to take place after centuries of exile in various nations around the world.

What do you learn about the end-times regathering of the Jews from Ezekiel 36:24?

Read Ezekiel 37:1-6. The coming together of bones, muscles, and flesh in this passage is a graphic metaphor about Israel's end-times restoration. How is Israel's rebirth as a nation like a resurrection from the dead?

These prophecies mean that 1948 is a year to remember. After all, in AD 70 Titus and his Roman warriors destroyed Jerusalem, ending Israel's identity as a political entity (see Luke 21:20). The Jews were dispersed worldwide for many centuries. In 1940, no one could have guessed that Israel would be a nation again within a decade. And yet it happened. Israel achieved statehood in 1948 (by God's miraculous providence), and Jews have been returning to their homeland ever since—primarily because of global anti-Semitism. All of this is in direct fulfillment of biblical prophecy.

Why do you think there continues to be such a high degree of anti-Semitism in the world today?

The event that begins the tribulation period will be the antichrist's signing of a covenant with Israel (Daniel 9:27). Can you see how Israel's national rebirth (with Jews returning to the land) is a *precondition* to the beginning of the tribulation period? Explain.

The Escalation of Apostasy

Another prophesied characteristic of the present age is the escalation of apostasy. The word *apostasy* comes from the Greek word *apostasia*, which means "falling away." The word refers to a falling away from the truth. It depicts a determined, willful defection from the faith or an abandonment of the faith.

Summarize what you learn about end-times apostasy from the following verses:

- 1 Timothy 4:1-2—

- 2 Timothy 3:1-8—

- 2 Timothy 4:3-4—

Can you think of specific ways some of these prophecies are being fulfilled in our own day? Jot down some examples here:

Apostasy will rise to a fever pitch during the tribulation period. In 2 Thessalonians 2:3, we are told: "Let no one deceive you in any way. For that day will not come, *unless the rebellion comes first.*" Many believe this refers to a rebellion against the truth.

Jesus Himself prophetically warns that during the tribulation period, "many will fall away…many false prophets will arise and lead many astray" (Matthew 24:9-12).

How can people know that so-called "prophets" are false? What specifically makes them *false?*

Why do you think God allows the emergence of "many false prophets"?

In what specific ways can we protect ourselves from the deceptions of false prophets?

The United States Will Apparently Weaken

There will be a major shift in the balance of power in the end times. The revived Roman Empire—a *United States of Europe*—will be headed by the antichrist, and this empire will apparently be the political and economic superpower at the first part of the tribulation period (see Daniel 2 and 7). Many prophecy scholars thus infer that the United States will progressively weaken by the time the tribulation begins. This is a strong possibility.

The question now becomes: *What might cause the United States to weaken?*

How does Job 12:23 indicate that God is sovereign over the nations?

How does Daniel 2:20-21 indicate that God is sovereign over the rise and fall of world leaders?

Read Romans 1:18-28. Do you think this passage applies to the current state of affairs in the United States? Might God judge the United States for gross moral failure?

Do you think the United States' demise could relate to a nuclear attack? An electromagnetic pulse (EMP) attack? A catastrophic cyber-attack? The rapture of the church? A combination of all these? Explain.

A Revived Roman Empire	
The antichrist will reign over it	Daniel 2 and 7
It will be composed of ten nations	Daniel 7:7, 19-20
The antichrist will start small but eventually will gain control over the entire empire	Daniel 7:7-8, 24; 2 Thessalonians 2:3-10; Revelation 13:1-10
The empire will be terrifying and powerful	Daniel 7:7; 2:40
The empire will not be wholly integrated	Daniel 2:41-43

LIFE LESSONS

Don't Trust Predictions Outside of the Bible

God has revealed the prophetic future to us through His prophets. Someone said that God *moved* and the prophets *mouthed* prophetic truths. God *revealed* and man *recorded* His words about the future (2 Peter 1:21; 2 Timothy 3:16; see also Acts 1:16; 4:24-26; Jeremiah 1:9; Zechariah 7:12). Trust no one else! Trust no other "holy book." And do not trust psychics, astrologers, and other occultists.

Obedience Brings Blessing

Let your study of prophecy motivate obedience to God. Obedience to God brings blessing (Luke 11:28), long life (1 Kings 3:14; John 8:51), happiness (Psalm 112:1; 119:56), peace (Proverbs 1:33), and a state of well-being (Jeremiah 7:23; see also Exodus 19:5; Leviticus 26:3-4; Deuteronomy 4:40; 12:28; 28:1; Joshua 1:8; 1 Chronicles 22:13; Isaiah 1:19). Look up these verses. *You'll be blessed.*

The Rebirth of Israel

Jews will be gathered from many nations—Ezekiel 36:24.

Ezekiel's vision of dry bones—Ezekiel 37:1-6.

Towns will be inhabited, ruins rebuilt—Ezekiel 36:10.

Will again be prosperous—Ezekiel 36:30.

End-Time Denials (Apostasy)

Authority—2 Timothy 3:4.

Christ—1 John 2:18; 4:3; 2 Peter 2:6.

Christ's return—2 Peter 3:3-4.

Christian liberty—1 Timothy 4:3-4.

Faith, the—1 Timothy 4:1-2; Jude 3.

God—Luke 17:26; 2 Timothy 3:4-5.

Morals—2 Timothy 3:1-8, 13; Jude 17-18.

Separated life—2 Timothy 3:1-7.

Sound doctrine—2 Timothy 4:3-4.

PRAYER ·

*My Father, my understanding that You have a specific purpose
and plan for both Israel and the church leads me to believe
that You have a specific plan for my life too. As I study prophecy,
please help me understand where I fit in the bigger scheme of
things and help me to perceive Your purpose for my life. I ask
that You also grant me spiritual discernment so that I might
avoid falling into any kind of false belief or apostasy. Keep me
strong in Scripture. Thank You in Jesus's name. Amen.*

Lesson 3

The Rapture

■ KEY CONCEPT

The rapture is that glorious event in which the dead in Christ will be resurrected and living Christians will be translated instantly into their glorified bodies. Both groups will be caught up to meet Christ in the air and taken back to heaven.

■ THE BIG IDEAS IN THIS LESSON

- The church—which includes all who have trusted in Christ for salvation since the day of Pentecost—will be raptured instantaneously and meet Christ in the air, thereafter relocating to heaven.
- This event precedes the tribulation period.
- This event is imminent—meaning it could take place at any moment.

■ PROBING THE SCRIPTURES

The Church Will Be Raptured

There will be one generation of Christians who will never pass through death's door. They will be alive on earth one moment. The next moment they will be with the Lord up in the air with glorified bodies. The dead in Christ will also be instantly resurrected. *What a moment that will be!*

What insights can you glean from the following Bible passages about the rapture?

- John 14:1-3—

- 1 Corinthians 15:51-55—

- 1 Thessalonians 4:13-17—

What excites you most about the rapture?

Some people are attacking the idea of the rapture today. Why do you think this is so?

The Rapture Is a "Mystery"

A mystery—as understood in Scripture—is a truth that was unknown to people living in Old Testament times but is now revealed to humankind by God. The word can also refer to a truth that cannot be discerned simply by human investigation but requires special revelation from God.

Read 1 Corinthians 15:51-55. What truths do you see in this passage that were not previously revealed in Old Testament times?

Though not explicitly revealed in the Old Testament, some people have speculated that there might be some *figurative allusions* to the rapture (and an escape from the tribulation period) in Old Testament Scripture. What do you think about the following verses in this regard? Be specific.

- Psalm 27:5—

- Psalm 57:1—

- Isaiah 26:20-21—

- Zephaniah 2:3—

Even if these verses do not specifically allude to the rapture, do you think the teachings of these verses show God's general desire to keep His people out of the "day of trouble"? How so?

We can say with certainty that no Old Testament verse affirms that countless people will disappear from the earth "in the twinkling of an eye" (1 Corinthians 15:52). Following the rapture, how do you think today's liberal media will report on the event?

The Voice of an Archangel

First Thessalonians 4:16 mentions "the voice of an archangel" in association with the rapture. Do you think the archangel Michael issues the command at the rapture? Or do you think Christ speaks with an archangel-like voice? (Scholars debate the issue.)

Read the following verses and write down a composite summary of the role of angels in the end times: 2 Thessalonians 1:7-8; Revelation 7:1-2; 8:1-6; 9:13-15; 12:7-9; 14:9-10; 15:1, 5-8; 16:1; 17:1; 21:9-12.

The Bridegroom and His Bride

Scripture portrays Christ as a divine Bridegroom (John 3:29) and the church as the bride of Christ (Revelation 19:7). The backdrop to this imagery is rooted in Hebrew weddings. There were three phases:

1. The marriage was legally consummated by the bride and groom's parents, after which the groom went to prepare a place to live in his father's house.

2. The bridegroom came to claim his bride at an unannounced time.

3. There was a marriage supper—a feast lasting several days.

All three of these phases are seen in Christ's relationship to the church:

1. As individuals living during the church age come to salvation, under the Father's loving and sovereign hand, they become a part of the bride of Christ (or the church). Meanwhile, Christ the Bridegroom is in heaven, preparing a place to live in the Father's house (John 14:1-3).

2. The Bridegroom (Jesus Christ) will come at an undisclosed time to claim His bride at the rapture. He will then take the bride back to heaven where He has prepared a place to live (John 14:1-3). The marriage ceremony will take place in heaven before the second coming (Revelation 19:6-16).

3. The marriage supper of the Lamb will be celebrated following the second coming.

There are additional parallels:

- Just as ancient Jewish grooms paid a purchase price to establish the marriage covenant, so Jesus paid a purchase price with His blood for the church (1 Corinthians 6:19-20; Acts 20:28).

- Just as a Jewish bride was declared "sanctified" or set apart in waiting for her groom, so the church has been declared sanctified and set apart

for Christ the Bridegroom (1 Corinthians 1:2; 6:11; Ephesians 5:25-27; Hebrews 10:10; 13:12).

- Just as a Jewish bride was unaware of the exact time her groom would come for her, so the church is unaware of the precise time Jesus the Bridegroom will arrive at the rapture, though it is an imminent event.

What does it mean to you personally that the Bridegroom (Jesus) could show up at any moment to take you to the place He has prepared in His Father's house? Be specific.

The Blessed Hope

The term "blessed hope" in Titus 2:13 refers to the rapture of the church. This event is blessed in the sense that it brings blessing to believers. The term carries the idea of *joyous anticipation*. Believers can hardly wait for it to happen!

Read Titus 2:13. How does Jesus's identity as "great God and Savior" make the rapture all the more blessed?

What else might make this a blessed event? (Take a look at 1 Corinthians 15:50-55.)

Some people claim the rapture happens *after* the tribulation period. How could the rapture be a "blessed hope" if it did not occur *before* the tribulation period, during which God's wrath will be poured out on the entire world? Explain.

Pretribulationism Is the Preferred View

Chronology clues in Scripture indicate that the rapture will take place before the tribulation period (and hence it is *pre*tribulational). This means the church will not go through the judgments prophesied in the book of Revelation (chapters 4–18). This view seems to be most consistent with a literal interpretation of biblical prophecy.

Read Revelation 3:10. Do you think the "hour of trial" mentioned in this verse is the future tribulation period described in Revelation 4–18? Explain.

When Jesus said, "I will keep you from the hour of trial that is coming on the whole world," the word *from* is the Greek word *ek*—meaning "separation from." Does Christ's "separation of" the church from the tribulation period sound like the rapture to you? Why or why not?

The following two indisputable facts are in keeping with the idea that the church will be raptured before the tribulation period:

1. No Old Testament passage on the tribulation period mentions the church (Deuteronomy 4:29-30; Jeremiah 30:4-11; Daniel 8:23-27; 12:1-2).

2. No New Testament passage on the tribulation period mentions the church (Matthew 13:24-30, 36-42, 47-50; 24:15-31; 1 Thessalonians 1:9-10; 5:4-10; 2 Thessalonians 2:1-12; Revelation 4–18).

The silence of Scripture regarding the church in the tribulation period points to the church's complete absence from this period.

Do you think Romans 5:9 refers to the rapture? Why or why not?

Read 1 Thessalonians 1:9-10. The Greek word for "delivers" in verse 10 literally means "to snatch out to oneself."

Do you think the phrase "to wait for his Son from heaven" in verse 10 refers to Christians awaiting the rapture as opposed to the second coming (after the tribulation period)? Explain.

How is the phrase "Jesus who delivers us [*snatches us*] from the wrath to come" consistent only with the pretribulational view?

In view of the "snatching up" in 1 Thessalonians 1:10 and believers being "caught up" to meet the Lord in the air in 1 Thessalonians 4:16-17, why do you think some Christians continue to deny that there is such a thing as the rapture?

We often witness God protecting His people before His judgment falls:

- Enoch was transferred to heaven before the judgment of the flood.

- Noah and his family were in the ark before the judgment of the flood.

- Lot was taken out of Sodom before judgment was poured out on Sodom and Gomorrah.

- The blood of the Passover lamb sheltered the firstborn among the Hebrews in Egypt before judgment fell.

- The spies were safely out of Jericho and Rahab was secured before judgment fell on Jericho.

How do these previous divine deliverances lend credence to the idea that God will rapture His people off the earth before His great wrath falls during the tribulation period? Explain.

God Protects His People	
God is our hiding place	Psalm 32:7
God is our refuge	Deuteronomy 33:27; Psalm 27:5; 31:20; 46:1
God protects us from the plots of the wicked	Psalm 64:2; 119:154; 140:1
Believers can dwell in the secret place of the Most High	Psalm 91:1
The Lord delivers believers out of trouble	Psalm 34:17-19; 121:8
The church will be delivered from the wrath to come	1 Thessalonians 1:10

Parallels Between Paul and Jesus

The apostle Paul's primary teaching on the rapture is in 1 Thessalonians 4:13-18. Jesus's primary teaching on the rapture is in John 14:2-3.

Read these two passages. List as many parallels as you can in two columns. After you go through this exercise, you can compare your findings with mine below.

Key Parallels

- *John 14:3 depicts Jesus as coming again to earth, which involves a descent from the heavenly realm.*
- First Thessalonians 4:16 likewise says Christ "will descend from heaven."
- *In John 14:3, Jesus says to believers that He "will take you to myself."*
- First Thessalonians 4:17 reveals that believers will be "caught up" to Christ.
- *John 14:3 reveals that believers will be with Christ ("where I am").*
- First Thessalonians 4:17 affirms that believers "will always be with the Lord."
- *John 14:1 contextually reveals that the purpose of this revelation about the rapture is that the hearts of Christ's followers will not be troubled.*
- First Thessalonians 4:13, 18 reveals that the purpose of this revelation about the rapture is to minimize grief and bring encouragement.

Given such similarities, we surmise that both passages refer to the same event—the rapture of the church, which takes place before the tribulation.

The Rapture Is Imminent

The term *imminent* means "ready to take place" or "impending." The New Testament teaches that the rapture is imminent—that is, there is nothing that must be prophetically fulfilled before the rapture occurs. It could happen at any moment.

What insights can you glean from the following verses about the imminence of the rapture?

- Philippians 3:20—

- Philippians 4:5—

- 1 Thessalonians 1:10—

- Titus 2:13—

- Jude 21—

Does the imminence of the rapture motivate increased commitment to the Lord?

The rapture is a *signless* event that can occur at any moment. This is in contrast to the second coming of Christ, which is preceded by many events or signs that transpire during the seven-year tribulation period (Revelation 4–18).

There will be one generation of Christians who will not pass through death's door. Do you think we might be that generation? Why or why not?

Write down the names of Christian loved ones you most look forward to seeing at the heavenly reunion that follows the rapture.

Does the fact that the rapture could occur at any moment give you a sense of urgency in evangelism?

LIFE LESSONS

Imminence and Righteousness

The imminence of the rapture ought to motivate us to live in purity and righteousness. Those expecting the Lord's soon return "will keep themselves pure, just as he is pure" (1 John 3:3 NLT). Because He could arrive at any moment, we are encouraged to live "holy and godly lives" (2 Peter 3:10-14 NLT; see also 1 Thessalonians 4:1-12; Romans 13:11-14).

Angels Among Us in the End Times

Angels are involved at both the rapture (1 Thessalonians 4:16) and the second coming (Matthew 25:31). But they are also intimately involved in each of our lives today. Angels are our guardians (Psalm 91:9-12; 2 Kings 6:17). God sometimes uses them in answering our prayers (Acts 12:5-11). They escort us into heaven if we die before the rapture (Luke 16:22). They minister to us in many and varied ways (Hebrews 1:13-14).

The Rapture Is Distinct from the Second Coming

- The Rapture: Christ will retrieve Christians from the earth and return to heaven—John 14:1-3.

- *The Second Coming: Christ will return to earth from heaven—Zechariah 14:4; Acts 1:9-11.*

- The Rapture: There is no judgment of the nations.

- *The Second Coming: Christ will judge all the nations—Matthew 25:31-46.*

- The Rapture: It is an imminent event; no signs precede it—1 Thessalonians 5:1-3.

- *The Second Coming: Many prophetic signs precede it—Luke 21:10-28; Revelation 4–18.*

- The Rapture: It occurs before the "day of wrath"—1 Thessalonians 1:10; 5:9.

- *The Second Coming: It occurs after the "day of wrath"—Revelation 19:11-16.*

- The Rapture: Christ comes *for* His bride—1 Thessalonians 4:16-17.

- *The Second Coming: Christ returns* with *His bride to earth—Revelation 19:6-14.*

PRAYER

> *Father, I rejoice in the reality that the rapture could occur at any moment. It excites me that Jesus could come for me before this very day is over. Because of that, I am motivated to live the way You want me to. I am encouraged to trust You. I am inspired to worship You. I am motivated to tell others about You. Father, keep me strong as I await the rapture. Please sustain me in righteous living until Christ comes for me. I can't wait. Thank You in Jesus's name. Amen.*

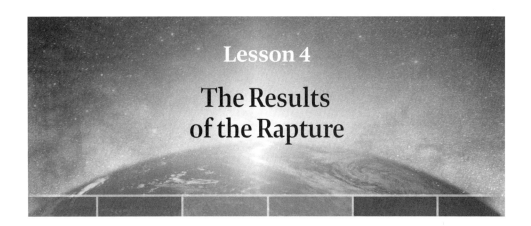

Lesson 4

The Results
of the Rapture

KEY CONCEPT

The two key results of the rapture are: (1) Christians will receive glorified bodies; and (2) the Holy Spirit's restraint of evil will be withdrawn from the earth.

THE BIG IDEAS IN THIS LESSON

- At the moment of the rapture, *all* Christians—dead or living—will receive "body upgrades." The dead will be instantly resurrected while the living will be instantly transformed and glorified. These new bodies will never age, get sick, or die.

- Following the rapture, the "Restrainer"—apparently the Holy Spirit—will no longer restrain evil on the earth. This will facilitate the easy emergence of the antichrist on the world stage.

PROBING THE SCRIPTURES

All Christians Will Receive "Body Upgrades"

We know with certainty that Jesus physically resurrected from the dead. Many witnesses attested that it really happened.

Consult the following verses and summarize the first-person testimony to Jesus's physical resurrection:

- Acts 2:32—

- Acts 3:15—

- Acts 10:39-41—

- 1 Corinthians 15:3-8—

- John 20:24-29—

Jesus's resurrection ensures *our* resurrection from the dead. Following Lazarus's death, Jesus promised Martha: "I am the resurrection and the life. Whoever believes in me, though he die, yet shall he live, and everyone who lives and believes in me shall never die" (John 11:25-26). To prove His authority to make this statement, Jesus raised Lazarus from the dead!

Read John 6:39-40. Summarize what the passage says about:

- The Father—

- The Son—

- The believer—

Imperishable and Glorious Bodies

Our body transformations will take place at the rapture. In an instant—*in the twinkling of an eye*—dead believers will be raised from the dead and the bodies of living Christians will be transformed into glorified bodies. All of us will then meet the Lord in the air (1 Thessalonians 4:13-17). From that moment forward, we will never again be subject to the frailties of weak mortal bodies. *No more sickness. No more death.*

What does the apostle Paul say about this in 1 Corinthians 15:42-44?

The reference to sowing is a symbolic reference to burial. Just as one sows a seed in the ground, the mortal body is "sown" in the sense that it is buried in the ground following death. When our bodies are placed in the grave, they decompose and return to dust.

The exciting news is that the decomposed bodies of dead believers will be gloriously resurrected. They will be raised *imperishable*. All liability to aging, disease, and death will be forever gone.

Do you presently have any bodily ailments? (List a few.)

How does 1 Corinthians 15:42-44 give you hope amid such bodily ailments?

Does Romans 8:18 alter your attitude about your present sufferings?

Scripture affirms that our present bodies—following death—are "sown in dishonor" (1 Corinthians 15:43).

In what way do you think it is dishonoring for the body to be buried?

We may bring some level of honor to a funeral service by dressing our dead loved ones in their best clothes, purchasing a nice-looking casket, displaying lots of beautiful flowers, and offering glowing eulogies. We should certainly do all of these things. But underlying it all is that death—despite our best efforts to camouflage it—is intrinsically dishonoring.

Contrary to such dishonor, our new bodies will be indescribably glorious. They will never again be subject to aging, decay, or death. Never again will our bodies be buried in the ground.

Try to imagine what it will be like after the rapture. You will be consciously aware that death and disease are *gone forever* and that you will *never again* age or have any symptoms of bodily decay. Jot down a few reflections on how freeing this awareness will be.

Our present bodies are characterized by weakness (1 Corinthians 15:43). From the moment we are born, "our outer self is wasting away" (2 Corinthians 4:16; see also 1:8-9). Vitality decreases, illness comes, and then old age follows with its wrinkles and decrepitude. Eventually, in old age, we may become increasingly incapacitated.

When you see young people who are full of energy and life, do you ever reflect on how you too used to be young, just like them? Jot down a few things that were easy to do in yesteryear, but you can no longer do.

Have you ever pondered how some of yesteryear's rich and glamorous movie stars look so old and weak today, or have already died? What does this tell you about the folly of living only for the things this world has to offer?

Do you agree with Christian leaders who say God uses the aging process to gently shift our priorities, turning our attention from this temporal world to the afterlife? Explain.

Both the rich and the poor die. Both males and females die. People of all colors die. Does this reality cause you to agree with the statement: "Death is the great equalizer"? Explain.

No More Weakness

Read 2 Corinthians 5:1-4. The apostle Paul likened our earthly bodies to tents and our future resurrection bodies to buildings. Two observations are noteworthy:

1. Paul was speaking in terms his Jewish listeners would have understood. The temporary tabernacle of Israel's wanderings in the wilderness was a giant tent-like structure, easy to tear down. It was eventually replaced with a permanent building in the Promised Land—a stone temple.

2. Similarly, the temporary "tent" (or body) in which believers now dwell will be replaced on the day of the rapture with an eternal, immortal, imperishable body, akin to a permanent building (1 Corinthians 15:42, 53-55).

What characteristics of a tent are similar to a mortal human body? Be creative. Try to think of several characteristics.

What characteristics of a stone building are similar to our future resurrection bodies? Again, be creative. Try to think of several characteristics.

Paul then says something we can all resonate with: *Our present bodies make us groan* (2 Corinthians 5:4)!

- When we get sick, we groan.

- As we age, we groan.

- As we face death, we groan.

To make 2 Corinthians 5:4 easier to understand, I've inserted some explanatory comments: "For while we are in this tent [*of our present mortal body that is aging*], we groan and are burdened, because we do not wish to be unclothed [*with the death of our mortal body*] but to be clothed instead with our heavenly dwelling [*our glorious resurrection body*], so that what is mortal [*our mortal and dying earthly body*] may be swallowed up by life [*our eternal resurrection body*]" (NIV).

Paul indicates that being "unclothed"—being without a physical body after death—is a state of incompletion and, for him, carries a sense of *nakedness* (2 Corinthians 5:2-4). Even though departing to be with Christ in a disembodied state is far better than life on earth (Philippians 1:21-23), Paul's true yearning was to be "clothed" with a physically resurrected body (2 Corinthians 5:4). That yearning will be fully satisfied at the rapture.

Meanwhile, during earthly life, we continue to groan because our "tents" are wearing down.

List a few things that make you groan about your present body.

Do you fear the time when your earthly tent will fall down in death? Explain your concerns specifically.

How does Jesus help you with this (Hebrews 2:14-15)?

What do you anticipate most about your future resurrection body?

The Holy Spirit: A Guarantee of What Is to Come

The apostle Paul affirmed that God has given us the Holy Spirit as *a deposit* of what is to come in the afterlife (2 Corinthians 5:5). Three things are important to remember:

1. The Greek word translated *deposit* was used among the Greeks to refer to a pledge that guaranteed final possession of an item.

2. The word was sometimes used of an engagement ring, which guaranteed that a marriage would take place.

3. The Holy Spirit is a "deposit" in the sense that His presence in our lives guarantees our eventual total transformation and glorification into the likeness of Christ's glorified resurrection body.

Why do you think God felt it necessary that we have the Holy Spirit as a "down payment" of our future glorification?

Though we are not bodily transformed yet, how is the Holy Spirit even now transforming our character (Galatians 5:16-23)?

Our Resurrection Bodies Will Be Physical

Here is something to think about: *Jesus's resurrection body was physical.* Five facts from the Bible assure us of this:

1. Jesus's body was missing from the tomb (Matthew 28:6; Mark 16:6; Luke 24:6).

2. The resurrected body was composed of flesh and bones (Luke 24:39).

3. People touched His resurrected body (Matthew 28:9; John 20:27-28).

4. The resurrected body was visible (Matthew 28:17).

5. Christ ate food after His resurrection (Luke 24:30, 40-42; John 21:12-13; Acts 1:4).

Since Philippians 3:21 affirms that our resurrection body will "be like his glorious body," describe some characteristics of our future resurrection body based on the above verses.

The "Restrainer" Will Be Removed

Another result of the rapture is that the "restrainer"—apparently God the Holy Spirit—will be removed, facilitating the easy emergence of the antichrist.

Read 2 Thessalonians 2:7-8. What two personalities are mentioned in this passage?

The *lawless one* in this passage is the antichrist. He will embody sin and promote it as it has never been promoted before. Everything about him will be rooted in sin.

The *restrainer* is apparently the Holy Spirit. How do we know this? Many theologians believe that only one person—the omnipotent God—is powerful enough to restrain Satan, who energizes the antichrist (2 Thessalonians 2:9). For this reason, they interpret the restrainer as being God the Holy Spirit, who Himself indwells the church.

Two key verses reveal that the Holy Spirit indwells the church:

- Summarize 1 Corinthians 3:16:

- Summarize 1 Corinthians 6:19:

Scripture also reveals the incredible power of the Holy Spirit:

How does 1 John 4:4 reveal that the Holy Spirit is more powerful than Satan, who energizes the antichrist?

The Greek word translated "restrain" in 2 Thessalonians 2:7-8 carries the idea:

- "to hold back from action"
- "to keep under control"
- "to shackle someone"

This is what the Holy Spirit does in our present day in preventing the Satan-energized antichrist from emerging on the scene.

Many believe the Holy Spirit accomplishes this restraint *through the church*. Here is their reasoning:

1. The Holy Spirit indwells each member of the church.

2. Indwelt by the all-powerful Holy Spirit, the church is divinely empowered to restrain evil in the world.

3. At the rapture, each member of the church is taken off the earth.

4. The restraining ministry of the Holy Spirit—as exercised through the worldwide church—thereby ceases at that moment.

5. This makes it easy for the antichrist to rise quickly on the world stage. It also makes it easy for the false world religion of the end times to emerge without resistance.

Does this five-point scenario seem feasible to you? Why or why not?

Here's an important qualification: Even though the Holy Spirit will be "out of the way" in terms of restraining evil, He will still carry out two key ministries:

1. He will be active in bringing people to salvation during the tribulation period (Revelation 7:9-12; John 16:7-11).

2. He will also empower and embolden His witnesses during that time (Revelation 7:1-4; 11:1-14; see also Mark 13:11; Acts 1:8; Philippians 4:3).

Anticipating the Resurrection Body

Scripture often speaks of the importance of meditating on Scripture as well as on God and His wondrous works (Joshua 1:8; Psalm 63:5-6; 119:15, 23, 48; 143:5). Meditate a few moments on God's future provision of a glorious resurrection body for you:

1. It will be an eternal body made by God Himself (2 Corinthians 5:1).
2. It will be a glorious body (Philippians 3:20-21).
3. It will be an imperishable body (1 Corinthians 15:42).
4. It will be a strong body (2 Corinthians 5:1).

Walking in the Spirit

The Holy Spirit not only restrains evil in the world, He also empowers us as Christians to overcome evil in our lives. In Galatians 5:16-17, the apostle Paul said: "Walk by the Spirit, and you will not gratify the desires of the flesh. For the desires of the flesh are against the Spirit, and the desires of the Spirit are against the flesh, for these are opposed to each other, to keep you from doing the things you want to do." *Walk* is present tense in the Greek, meaning continuous action. We are to walk in the Spirit 24/7.

Evidence for Christ's Resurrection

Jesus appeared to the disciples—John 20:19.
Jesus showed the disciples His hands and side—John 20:20.
The resurrection accounts for the apostles' fearless witness—Acts 5:27-32.
Jesus appeared to Saul (Paul)—Acts 9.
Jesus appeared to his brother James—John 7:5; 1 Corinthians 15:7.
Doubting Thomas became convinced—John 20:24-29.
Jesus gave many convincing proofs over forty days—Acts 1:3.
Jesus appeared to over five hundred at the same time—1 Corinthians 15:6.

Believers Will Be Resurrected

We will receive new bodies—2 Corinthians 5:1-4; Philippians 3:21.

The perishable body will become imperishable—1 Corinthians 15:42-44.

Resurrection will swallow up death—Isaiah 25:8.

We will all be changed—1 Corinthians 15:50-52.

PRAYER ·

> *Father, how awesome it is to ponder that while our present bodies
> are weak, our glorified bodies will be strong. While our present
> bodies are mortal and perishable, our glorified bodies will be
> immortal and imperishable. While our present bodies are subject
> to disease and death, our glorified bodies will be eternally healthy
> and death-free. To think that the rapture is imminent and that I
> could have a new body by the end of the day, WOW! Thank You for
> making this possible for me. Thank You in Jesus's name. Amen.*

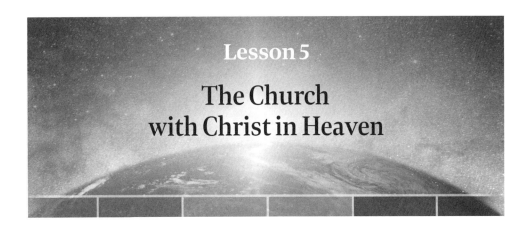

Lesson 5

The Church with Christ in Heaven

◼ KEY CONCEPT

Two key events occur once the church is in heaven: the judgment seat of Christ and the marriage of the lamb.

◼ THE BIG IDEAS IN THIS LESSON

- Following the rapture, Christians in heaven will face the judgment seat of Christ. They will either receive rewards from Christ or suffer the loss of such rewards, based on how they lived from the moment they first became Christians.

- The church is the bride of Christ. The church as a bride in heaven will experience the marriage of the Lamb with the divine Bridegroom, Jesus Christ.

◼ PROBING THE SCRIPTURES

Christians Will Face Christ in Judgment

Believers will one day stand before the judgment seat of Christ—also called "the Bema." Each believer's life will be examined regarding deeds done during earthly life. Personal motives and intents of the heart will also be weighed.

What does Hebrews 4:13 tell us about the penetrating scrutiny of our divine Judge?

How does this verse motivate Christians to deal with so-called "secret sins"?

The athletic games of the apostle Paul's day give us insights on the nature of a judgment seat. Upon completion of a game, a dignitary would sit upon a judgment seat and dispense rewards to the winning athletes—usually a wreath of leaves, which was considered a victor's crown. As Christians, you and I will stand before Christ's judgment seat and receive (*or possibly lose*) rewards.

This judgment will not occur in a corporate setting, like a big class being praised or scolded by a teacher. Instead, it will be individual and personal.

Read Romans 14:10-12.

- What does this passage reveal about what will take place at this judgment?

- Do you feel prepared to "give an account" of your life to God? Why or why not? (*This is a scary question for each of us. But it's spiritually healthy for us to consider it.*)

This judgment has nothing to do with whether Christians will remain saved. Those who have placed faith in Christ *are* saved, and nothing threatens that. Believers are *eternally secure* in their salvation.

What do you learn about the security of your salvation from the following Bible passages?

- John 10:28-30—

- Romans 8:29-30—

- Romans 8:31-39—

- Ephesians 1:13-14—

- Ephesians 4:30—

- Hebrews 7:25—

Construct a single sentence affirming why you believe in eternal security based on the verses above.

Read 1 Corinthians 3:12-15 to gain further insights about the future judgment of Christians.

What do you think might be meant by gold, silver, precious stones, wood, hay, and straw?

What do you make of the fact that the materials Paul mentions are combustible in increasing degrees?

Some of these materials are useful for building, while others are not. What is the significance of this as related to judgment?

Is it possible that some of these materials may represent things of lasting significance, while others may represent things of rapidly fading value? Why or why not?

If your works were tested by fire today, how do you think you would fare? In what areas might you fall short?

Do you think such verses might be intended to "scare us straight"? Explain.

What does this passage tell you about the security of our salvation?

Avoid Shame

I hate to ponder the possibility. Some believers may experience a sense of deprivation, forfeiture, and shame at the judgment seat of Christ. Some rewards may be forfeited that otherwise might have been received. This will involve a sense of loss.

What is your reaction to the exhortation in 2 John 8? Be specific.

Are there any areas in your life right now where you may need to "watch yourself"? Explain.

As scary as some of this may sound, let's keep in mind a word picture from Tony Evans: *We can't erase what's already been recorded on God's camera, but we can start recording new and better footage today.*

It's also important to keep a balanced understanding of Scripture. While some will fare better than others at the judgment seat of Christ, *all* Christians will be in heaven, and *all* Christians will dwell face-to-face with Christ forever! Christ's coming for us at the rapture and the prospect of living eternally with Him is therefore something that should give each of us great joy. And that joy will last for all eternity.

The Scope of the Judgment Will Include Actions

The judgment seat of Christ will focus on the Christian's stewardship of the gifts, talents, opportunities, and responsibilities given to him or her in this present earthly life. The character of each Christian's life and service will be laid bare by Christ's omniscient vision (Revelation 1:14). Nothing will escape His notice.

Numerous Scripture verses reveal that each of our actions will be judged before the Lord.

Summarize what you learn from the following verses:

- Psalm 62:11-12—

- Matthew 16:27—

- Ephesians 6:5-8—

The Scope of the Judgment Will Include Thoughts

Summarize what you learn from the following verses about how our innermost thoughts will come under the Lord's penetrating scrutiny:

- Jeremiah 17:10—

- 1 Corinthians 4:5—

The Scope of the Judgment Will Include Words

Summarize what you learn from the following verses about how the words we speak will come under judgment:

- Matthew 12:36-37—

- James 3:1-12—

The Judgment Seat of Christ Will Follow the Rapture

Scripture hints that the judgment seat of Christ will occur immediately after the rapture when Christ takes the saints back to heaven. No Bible verse explicitly states this. However, the twenty-four elders in heaven mentioned in Revelation 4 apparently represent church-age believers. Notice that they are portrayed as *already having received* their crowns in heaven at the start of the tribulation period (see 2 Timothy 4:8; James 1:12; 1 Peter 5:4; Revelation 2:10). This leads us to believe they have *already experienced* the judgment seat of Christ, where such crowns will be handed out. This means the judgment of believers must take place soon after the rapture.

Rewards—Crowns

The rewards Christians will receive at the judgment seat of Christ are described as crowns. These various crowns symbolize the various spheres of achievement and award in the Christian's life.

What do you learn about these crowns from the following verses?

- James 1:12—

- Revelation 2:10—

- 1 Peter 5:1-4—

- 1 Corinthians 9:24-25—

- 2 Timothy 4:8—

The Judgment of Christians	
Nature of	**Scripture**
Universal	"We will *all* stand before the judgment seat of God" (Romans 14:10).
Knowledge	The extent of one's knowledge of God's will is considered (Luke 12:48).
Works	"You repay all people according to what they have done" (Psalm 62:12 NLT).
Thoughts	"I am the one who searches out the thoughts…I will give to each of you whatever you deserve" (Revelation 2:23 NLT).
Words	"You must give an account on judgment day for every idle word you speak" (Matthew 12:36 NLT).
Salvation Is Secure	"If the work is burned up, the builder will suffer great loss. The builder will be saved" (1 Corinthians 3:15 NLT).
Run the Race	Christians should seek to run the race well so they can obtain "the prize" (1 Corinthians 9:24-25).

The Marriage of the Lamb Takes Place

Scripture describes the church as a virgin bride awaiting the soon coming of her heavenly Bridegroom (2 Corinthians 11:2). Jesus Himself is the heavenly Bridegroom (Matthew 9:15; 22:1-14; 25:1-13; Mark 2:18-20; Luke 5:33-35; 14:15-24; John 3:29). While awaiting the coming of her Groom, the bride of Christ seeks to keep herself pure, unstained from the world.

Read Revelation 19:6-9. Is your lifestyle befitting a bride who is awaiting the soon appearance of her Bridegroom?

If the rapture were to happen in the next hour, what areas of your life might make you feel unprepared for the event? Are there any areas that might cause some level of shame?

Are there any midcourse corrections you want to make in your life today?

LIFE LESSONS

Live for the Line

In his book *Seeing the Unseen: A Daily Dose of Eternal Perspective*, Randy Alcorn exhorts: "Life on earth is a dot, a brief window of opportunity; life in Heaven (and ultimately on the New Earth) is a line going out from that dot for eternity. If we're smart, we'll live not for the *dot*, but for the *line*." The more successfully we live for the line, the better our prospects will be at the future judgment seat of Christ.

Fear of the Lord

The prospect of the future judgment seat of Christ naturally leads to a healthy fear of the Lord. Fear of the Lord motivates one to be obedient to God (Deuteronomy 5:29; Ecclesiastes 12:13-14) and avoid evil (Proverbs 3:7; 8:13; 16:6). Fear of the Lord is true wisdom (Job 28:28; Psalm 111:10) and the beginning of knowledge (Proverbs 1:7). God blesses those who fear Him (Psalm 115:13). Fear of the Lord leads to riches, honor, and long life (Proverbs 22:4). God shows mercy to those who fear Him (Luke 1:50). A person who fears the Lord need not fear anything else.

God Can Restore Our Lives

If you're feeling threatened by the future judgment seat of Christ and feel that

maybe you need restoration to the Lord, I've got good news for you. *God is in the business of restoring lives.* Remember what David affirmed so long ago:

> The LORD is my shepherd; I shall not want.
>> He makes me lie down in green pastures.
>> He leads me beside still waters.
>>> *He restores my soul*
>>> (Psalm 23:1-3).

God can certainly restore the joy of your salvation. Pray along with the psalmist: "*Restore to me* the joy of your salvation" (Psalm 51:12).

God can also restore us after we've experienced hard trials: "After you have suffered a little while, the God of all grace, who has called you to his eternal glory in Christ, will himself *restore, confirm, strengthen, and establish you*" (1 Peter 5:10; see also Psalm 71:20).

Don't give up. If you feel down and out, God can restore you. Turn to Him today. *Delay is your enemy.* God can bring you back to His green pastures this very day.

DIGGING DEEPER WITH CROSS-REFERENCES

Our Assurance of Salvation

Our assurance is based on Scripture—1 John 5:10-13.

We are given assurance from Christ Himself—John 5:24.

God can keep us from falling—Jude 24.

God guards what we entrust to Him—2 Timothy 1:12.

The Holy Spirit testifies that we are God's children—Romans 8:16.

Jesus constantly intercedes for us—Hebrews 7:25.

Nothing can separate us from God—Romans 8:38-39.

We are secure in the Father's hands—John 10:29.

We are sealed by the Holy Spirit for the day of redemption—Ephesians 4:30.

We can be confident of our salvation—Ephesians 3:11-12.

The Judgment Seat of Christ

Believers are judged for things done in the body—2 Corinthians 5:10.

Believers must "run" to win the prize—1 Corinthians 9:24-27.

Believers will stand before the judgment seat—Romans 14:8-10.

Believers' works will be tested by fire—1 Corinthians 3:10-15.

Christ's eyes discern all—Revelation 1:14.

Each person will be rewarded according to his or her works—Psalm 62:11-12;

Matthew 16:27; Ephesians 6:5-8.

The Lord examines the mind, heart, and conduct—Jeremiah 17:10; Revelation 2:23.

The Lord will bring our motives to light—1 Corinthians 4:5.

The Lord will judge our words—Matthew 12:35-37.

Some believers may be ashamed at Christ's coming—1 John 2:28.

Some believers may lose rewards but still be saved—1 Corinthians 3:15; 2 John 8.

Crowns—Future Rewards

The crown incorruptible: For those who maintain self-control—1 Corinthians 9:25.

The crown of glory: For those who minister God's Word to God's flock—1 Peter 5:4.

The crown of life: For those who persevere under trial—James 1:12; Revelation 2:10.

The crown of righteousness: For those who long for the second coming—2 Timothy 4:8.

Believers will lay their crowns before God's throne—Revelation 4:9-11.

Some believers may lose crowns—2 John 8.

PRAYER

Father, how awesome it is to ponder that one day I will be with You in heaven. When I face Jesus at the judgment seat, how I long to receive a reward from Him. I so often feel unworthy as a Christian—and unworthy of any reward at all. But it would thrill me to no end to receive some reward for something I did right, even if feebly done. As part of the bride of Christ, please grant me a special grace to remain in complete fidelity to my Lord Jesus—my Groom—as I await His arrival at the rapture. I want to be ready. I don't want to shrink back in shame at His judgment. Thank You in Jesus's name. Amen.

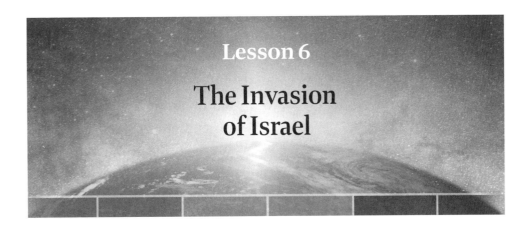

Lesson 6

The Invasion of Israel

▪ KEY CONCEPT

A powerful northern military coalition will invade Israel in the end times—possibly after the rapture, but before the tribulation period.

▪ THE BIG IDEAS IN THIS LESSON

- A precondition to Israel being invaded is that she must be living in relative security—a condition that is arguably true today.

- This condition met, Israel will be invaded by a powerful northern military coalition made up of Russia, Iran, Turkey, Sudan, Libya, and other Muslim nations. This invasion may take place after the rapture but before the tribulation period.

▪ PROBING THE SCRIPTURES

Israel Will Live in Security in the Land

The prophet Ezekiel, some 2600 years ago, prophesied that the Jews would be regathered from nations around the world back to the land of Israel in the end times (Ezekiel 36–37). Sometime after this, he said, there would be an all-out invasion of Israel by a massive northern assault force composed of Russia, Iran, Turkey, Sudan, Libya, and other Muslim nations. The goal of the assault force will be to obliterate the Jews. Given the overwhelming size of the assault force, Israel will have no chance of defending herself.

Ezekiel's prophecy stipulates that a precondition for this end-time invasion is that Israel must be living in relative security.

What evidence do you find for Israel living in security in the following verses, in which Ezekiel brings God's words to those who will invade Israel?

- Ezekiel 38:8—

- Ezekiel 38:10-11—

This invasion by the northern military coalition *cannot occur* until this state of security exists for Israel. But what brings about this sense of security? Bible expositors debate the issue. There are two primary interpretive scenarios.

Scenario 1: Security in Israel Is a Present Reality

Some prophecy teachers believe Israel is already in a state of relative security. They suggest this security is rooted in the following factors:

- Israel has peace treaties with some of the nations in the Middle East.
- Israel has a well-equipped army.
- Israel has a first-rate air force.
- Israel has an effective missile-defense system.
- Israel has a robust economy.
- Israel has historically maintained a strong relationship with the United States.

Does this scenario seem feasible to you? Why or why not?

Scenario 2: Security in Israel Will Be a Future Reality

A second scenario views Israel as being on constant high alert because of her close vicinity to her often-hostile Arab and Muslim neighbors. Since Israel became a nation in 1948, there has never been a time when Israel has been able to let her guard down.

Advocates of this scenario suggest that Israel will experience security only when the leader of a revived Roman Empire—the antichrist—signs a covenant with Israel at the beginning of the tribulation period (Daniel 9:27). From the moment the antichrist signs the covenant—and on through the next three-and-a-half years—Israel will enjoy a heightened sense of security.

Does this scenario seem feasible to you? Why or why not?

Two Scenarios—Two Chronologies

There are good prophecy scholars who hold to each of the two scenarios above. Both views are feasible. But both views involve different prophetic chronologies:

Scenario 1 Chronology

- Israel is presently in a state of security, primarily based on her military might.

- This security does not depend on the antichrist's signing of the covenant with Israel.

- Therefore, the invasion of the northern military coalition could take place at any time, even before the tribulation period begins.

Scenario 2 Chronology

- Israel's state of security depends on the antichrist's signing of the covenant with Israel—a signing that constitutes the beginning of the tribulation period.

- This means the invasion of Israel cannot occur *until* the tribulation period begins.

My Assessment

I believe Israel is already in a state of relative security. I also believe the invasion will likely take place sometime *after the rapture* but *before the tribulation period*. (Keep in mind that there could be years between the rapture and the tribulation period.) There are five factors that convince me of this view:

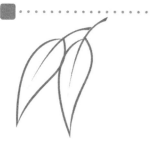

1. The rapture will likely cause worldwide chaos. The chaos will likely be greatly escalated in the United States because of its heavy population of Christians. The rapture will probably devastate the economy of the United States since so many of its workers will be gone. This being the case, Russia and its Muslim allies may seize the moment and consider this the ideal time to strike against Israel.

2. God will then utterly destroy the Russian and Muslim invaders prior to the tribulation period. This power vacuum may, in turn, open the door for the rapid rise of the antichrist as the leader of a revived Roman Empire—a European superstate.

3. The destruction of the Muslim invaders prior to the tribulation period might make it easier for the antichrist to sign a peace pact with Israel at the beginning of the tribulation period (Daniel 9:27). Israel will be much easier to protect.

4. It will be far easier for Israel to construct the Jewish temple on the Temple Mount in Jerusalem with Muslim forces having been decimated.

5. If the invasion takes place after the rapture, and the rapture takes place at least three-and-a-half years before the beginning of the tribulation period, then this scenario would allow for the weapons used in the invasion to be completely burned for seven years (Ezekiel 39:9-10) *before* the midpoint of the tribulation, when the Jews are forced to take sudden flight from Jerusalem (Matthew 24:15-21).

Does this scenario seem feasible to you? Why or why not?

If you disagree with this scenario, when do you believe the invasion will occur? And why?

The Nations in the Northern Military Coalition

The prophet Ezekiel clues us in on the identity of the nations that comprise the

northern military coalition that will invade Israel (Ezekiel 38:1-6). The invading nations include:

- *Rosh*, which likely refers to modern Russia, to the uttermost north of Israel.

- *Magog*, which refers to the geographical area in the southern portion of the former Soviet Union—probably including the former southern Soviet republics of Kazakhstan, Kyrgyzstan, Uzbekistan, Turkmenistan, Tajikistan, and possibly even northern parts of modern Afghanistan.

- *Meshech and Tubal*, which refers to the geographical territory to the south of the Black and Caspian Seas of Ezekiel's day, which is modern Turkey.

- *Persia*, which refers to modern Iran. Persia became Iran in 1935 and the Islamic Republic of Iran in 1979.

- *Ethiopia*, which refers to the geographical territory to the south of Egypt on the Nile River—what is today known as Sudan.

- *Put*, a land to the west of Egypt, which is modern-day Libya. The term may also include the modern-day countries of Algeria and Tunisia.

- *Gomer*, which refers to a part of the geographical territory in modern Turkey.

- *Beth-togarmah*, which also apparently refers to modern-day Turkey, though may also include Azerbaijan and Armenia.

The unique alignment of these nations as described in Ezekiel 38:1-6 has never occurred in the past. *But it is happening in our day.*

Some have suggested that maybe this invasion already took place back in Bible times. How do the phrases "latter years" (Ezekiel 38:8) and "latter days" (Ezekiel 38:16) argue against this view?

Do you think the fact that we are seeing this unique alignment of nations in our day indicates we are living in the end times? Why or why not?

An alliance between many of the nations mentioned in Ezekiel 38:1-6 may not have made good sense in Ezekiel's day since these nations are not even located next to each other.

> How does an alliance between these distant nations now make more sense, given the emergence of Islam in the seventh century AD—long after Ezekiel's prophecy was written? Explain.

The Debate Over the Term "Rosh"

Many have wondered: Why does the term "Rosh" not appear in many modern translations except as a marginal reading?

- The Hebrew word in this verse can be taken as either a proper noun (a geographical place called Rosh) or as an adjective (meaning "chief").

- If it's an adjective, it qualifies the meaning of the word "prince," so that it is translated "*chief* prince."

- I believe the renowned Hebrew scholars C.F. Keil and Wilhelm Gesenius are correct in saying Rosh refers to a geographical place.

- The translation of Rosh as an adjective ("*chief* prince") can be traced to the Latin Vulgate, translated by Jerome—who himself admitted that he did not base his translation on grammatical considerations.

- Jerome resisted translating Rosh as a proper noun simply because he could not find it mentioned as a geographical place anywhere else in Scripture.

- Many modern English translations have followed Jerome on this verse.

- Taking Rosh as a geographical place is the most natural rendering of the original Hebrew.

- There is no legitimate linguistic reason for taking it as an adjective.

Some may wonder, how does this debate relate to our prophetic understanding of the invading force against Israel? It comes down to this:

1. If the Hebrew term for Rosh is a geographical place (Russia), then both Russia and a group of Muslim nations will attack Israel. (This is my view.)

2. If the Hebrew term for Rosh is an adjective ("chief prince"), then a group of Muslim nations will attack Israel (with no involvement from Russia). Either way, Israel will be attacked by an overwhelming coalition of nations.

No Allies Will Come to Israel's Rescue

Martin Luther once said, "One plus God is a majority." We can apply this maxim to the Ezekiel invasion. Israel will stand alone—*with no allies*—when attacked by the massive northern military coalition (Ezekiel 38:10-13). This means the odds of Israel's survival—from a strictly human perspective—will be nil. Israel will be overwhelmingly outgunned. If this were a mere human battle, the outcome would be easy to predict.

However, God is almighty—and "one plus God is a majority." Ezekiel 38–39 reveals that our all-powerful God will annihilate the invading forces before any damage falls upon Israel.

What do you learn about God's power from the following verses?

- Jeremiah 32:17—

- Psalm 147:5—

- 2 Chronicles 20:5-6—

- Daniel 4:34-35—

- Isaiah 43:13—

- Psalm 24:8—

Scripture also reveals that God is always watchful over Israel. What do you learn about this from the following verses?

• Psalm 121:3-4—

• Isaiah 54:17—

Read Ezekiel 38:18-19. What words describe God's attitude toward the northern military invaders?

God's multifaceted defeat of the northern military coalition is an awesome thing to ponder. Read Ezekiel 38:19-23 and summarize what God will do to the invaders:

Ezekiel 38:21 reveals that God will sovereignly induce the various nations' armies in the invading force to turn on each other and kill each other. There are two scenarios that make good sense:

1. The armies who turn on each other all speak different languages—including Russian, Farsi, Arabic, and Turkic. Communication will break down and infighting will erupt.

2. The Russians and Muslim nations turn on each other—mutually suspecting a double cross.

Which of these scenarios do you think is more likely—and why?

Do you think it possible that both scenarios might unfold at the same time?

What does it say about God's sovereign power that He is able to control human beings in this way? (Proverbs 21:1 may help you.)

Do you perhaps have a different interpretive scenario of why these various armies turn on each other? If so, explain here:

God also promises: "I will send fire on Magog and on those who dwell securely in the coastlands" (Ezekiel 39:6). As noted previously, the term *Magog* refers to the geographical area in the southern part of the former Soviet Union, including the former Soviet republics of Kazakhstan, Kyrgyzstan, Uzbekistan, Turkmenistan, Tajikistan, and possibly even northern parts of modern Afghanistan. God will rain down fire upon this area of the world, as well as Magog's allies "who dwell securely in the coastlands"—both Russian and Muslim.

Do you think this fire will involve nuclear weaponry or fire directly from God? Why?

Do you agree with Joel Rosenberg who suggests that the object of this fire will include enemy nuclear missile silos, military bases, radar installations, defense ministries, intelligence headquarters, as well as Islamic mosques, madrassas, and schools?

Enemy Bodies—Collected and Buried

The burial of enemy bodies will begin immediately after God destroys the northern military alliance. The number of slain invaders will be staggering. Casualties will be so vast that only a deep valley will suffice for all the corpses (Ezekiel 39:11). It will take seven months to bury all the bodies in this valley.

Following the seven months, a secondary burial crew will traverse the land as they engage in a mopping up operation. They will search with precision for any bones that were missed.

Consult Numbers 19:11-22. Summarize why, from a Jewish perspective, it will be critically important for *all* body parts to be discovered and then buried in the ground.

Enemy Weapons—Gathered and Burned

There will be a shortage of burnable materials in the tribulation period. Revelation 8:7 reveals that "a third of the earth was burned up, and a third of the trees were burned up, and all green grass was burned up." One can easily understand why the Jews will find it necessary to gather and burn enemy weapons for seven years.

We can make two observations relating to prophetic chronology:

1. If the Ezekiel invasion occurs at least three-and-a-half years before the beginning of the tribulation period, the burning of weapons will be completed by the midpoint of the tribulation period.

2. This is important because the Jews will be forced to escape Jerusalem with great haste at the midpoint of the tribulation when the antichrist sets up headquarters there (Matthew 24).

A Testimony to God's Greatness

God will give a worldwide testimony of His power and glory in destroying the northern military coalition.

What do the following verses reveal about God's global testimony?

• Ezekiel 38:23—

- Ezekiel 39:7—

- Ezekiel 39:21-22—

How are God's words especially significant given that the Muslim invaders will likely be shouting *Allahu Akbar* ("Allah is the greatest") as they attack Israel? Explain.

LIFE LESSONS ·

God Is Sovereign over All Human History

God is sovereign over human affairs. God rules the universe, controls all things, and is Lord over all (Ephesians 1). All forms of existence are within the scope of His absolute dominion. God asserts, "My counsel shall stand, and I will accomplish all my purpose" (Isaiah 46:10). God assures us, "As I have planned, so shall it be, and as I have purposed, so shall it stand" (Isaiah 14:24). I encourage you to allow your life to *rest* in the sovereignty of God, no matter what you are facing.

God Controls the Nations

Scripture reveals that God "makes nations great, and he destroys them; he enlarges nations, and leads them away" (Job 12:23). He sovereignly determines which nations should rise and fall (Acts 17:25-26). Keep these verses in mind whenever the evening news reports on turmoil among the nations of the world. *God is always in control!*

DIGGING DEEPER WITH CROSS-REFERENCES · · · · · · · · · · · ·

God Fights for His People

"The LORD will fight for you, and you have only to be silent"—Exodus 14:14.

"You shall not fear them, for it is the LORD your God who fights for you"—Deuteronomy 3:22.

"Do not fear or panic or be in dread of them, for the LORD your God is he who goes with you to fight for you against your enemies, to give you the victory"—Deuteronomy 20:3-4.

God Is Our Protector

The Lord protects those who love Him—Psalm 145:20.

The Lord protects those who walk with integrity—Proverbs 2:7.

God protects His people from the plots of the wicked—Psalm 64:2; 119:154.

The Lord can protect us from violent people—Psalm 140:1-2.

God can use angels to guard and protect His people—Psalm 91:11; Matthew 18:10.

PRAYER

Father, You truly are a promise-keeping God. So far, You've kept every promise You made to Israel. That sets a precedent for the promises yet to be fulfilled to Israel. You've promised to protect Israel, saying, "He who keeps Israel will neither slumber nor sleep," and "no weapon that is fashioned against you shall succeed." Your covenant people are secure in Your hands. I, as a Gentile believer, am also secure in Your hands. I praise You for that. Thank You in Jesus's name. Amen.

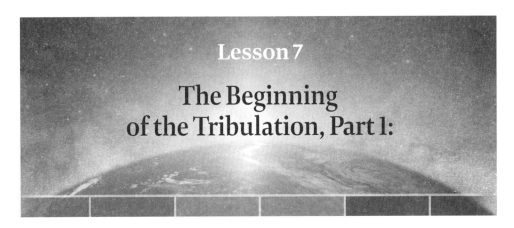

Lesson 7

The Beginning
of the Tribulation, Part 1:

Emergence of the Antichrist

KEY CONCEPT

The tribulation period will begin when the antichrist signs a covenant with Israel. He will then rise rapidly on the world stage.

THE BIG IDEAS IN THIS LESSON

- The antichrist—the head of a revived Roman Empire—will sign a covenant with Israel. This signing will mark the beginning of the tribulation period. He will apparently solve the Middle East conflict and guarantee protection for Israel.

- The antichrist will be an intellectual, commercial, military, oratorical, and political genius. He will rise rapidly on the world stage. He will perform counterfeit signs and wonders, and will seduce the world into submitting to his diabolical rule.

PROBING THE SCRIPTURES

The Antichrist Will Sign a Covenant

We read about the antichrist's covenant with Israel in the context of the "seventy weeks of Daniel." The following bullet points are a mini-crash course on the seventy weeks:

- Israel's prophetic timetable in Daniel 9 is divided into seventy groups of seven years, totaling 490 years.

- The first sixty-nine groups of seven years—or 483 years—counted the years "from the going out of the word to restore and build Jerusalem to the coming of an anointed one" (Daniel 9:25).

- The "anointed one" is Jesus, the Messiah. The day Jesus rode into Jerusalem to proclaim Himself Israel's Messiah was precisely 483 years to the day after the Persian King Artaxerxes had given the command to restore and rebuild Jerusalem.

- *At that point, God's prophetic clock stopped.*

- Daniel describes a gap between these 483 years and the final seven years of Israel's prophetic timetable. During this gap, Daniel's prophecy says three things will happen:

  1. The Messiah will be killed.

  2. The city of Jerusalem and its temple will be destroyed. (This occurred in AD 70.)

  3. The Jews would then encounter difficulty and hardship from that time forward.

- The final "week" of seven years will begin for Israel when the antichrist signs a seven-year covenant.

Read Daniel 9:27. How long is the covenant intended to last?

Why do you think the covenant is called a "strong covenant"?

Why will the antichrist put an end to the Jewish temple sacrifices after three-and-a-half years?

The Day of the Lord

There are two "beginnings" associated with the antichrist's signing of a covenant with Israel:

1. The beginning of the tribulation period.

2. The beginning of the day of the Lord.

The term "day of the Lord" is used in several senses in Scripture. Let's consider both the Old and New Testaments:

The Old Testament prophets used "day of the Lord" in two ways:

1. It was sometimes used of an event to be fulfilled in the near future.

2. It was sometimes used of the future tribulation period.

The immediate context of the term indicates which sense is intended. In all cases, God is viewed as actively intervening supernaturally to bring judgment against sin in the world. It is a time when God controls and dominates history in a direct way.

The New Testament is consistent in using "day of the Lord" to identify the judgment that will climax in the tribulation period (2 Thessalonians 2:2; Revelation 16–18), as well as the judgment that will usher in the new earth in the more distant end times (2 Peter 3:10-13; Revelation 20:7–21:1; see also Isaiah 65:17-19; 66:22). This theme of judgment against sin runs like a thread through all the references to the day of the Lord.

Here is an *If-Then* question to ponder:

If the day of the Lord involves God actively intervening supernaturally in the world—and *if* this "day" embraces not just the tribulation period but also runs through the time when God creates a new earth after the millennial kingdom—*then* what does this say about God's *steady and continuous* involvement in end-time events? Explain.

The Antichrist Rises on the World Stage

Though sin and lawlessness are already pervasive in our present world (2 Thessalonians 2:7), prophecy warns that a day is coming in which a specific individual—a "man of lawlessness," or *the antichrist*—will rise to power during the tribulation who will actually embody sin and lawlessness (2 Thessalonians 2:3-9; see also 1 John 2:18; Revelation 11:7; 13:1-10).

The word *antichrist* is made up of two words: *anti* and *Christ*. The Greek word for *anti* means "against" and "instead of." What does this reveal about the nature of the antichrist?

What two titles are ascribed to the antichrist in 2 Thessalonians 2:3? What do these two titles reveal about the antichrist's character?

Read 2 Thessalonians 2:3-12. What observations can you make about the "man of lawlessness" from this passage?

What interesting choice of words are used in Daniel 8:23 to describe the antichrist's great intellect?

How do the prophetic books of Daniel and Revelation indicate the antichrist's economic acumen (Daniel 11:43; Revelation 13:16-17)?

How is the antichrist's military ability described in Revelation 6:2?

How is the antichrist's self-exaltation indicated in Daniel 11:36?

How is the political influence of the antichrist evident in Revelation 17:12-13?

The antichrist will perform counterfeit signs and wonders and deceive countless people during the tribulation period (2 Thessalonians 2:9-10). The apostle John describes him as "the beast" (Revelation 13:1-10).

Describe your initial impressions about contrasts between *the beast* (the antichrist) and *the Lamb* (Jesus).

Though the antichrist initially appears benevolent with his covenant with Israel (Daniel 9:27), his true colors surface as the tribulation period unfolds. He will seek to dominate the world, adopt an anti-God agenda, double-cross and then seek to destroy the Jews, persecute believers, and set up his own kingdom on earth (Revelation 13). He will speak arrogant and boastful words in glorifying himself (2 Thessalonians 2:4).

The antichrist's assistant, the false prophet, will seek to make the world worship the antichrist (Revelation 13:11-12). He will enforce the "mark of the beast," without which people cannot buy or sell (Revelation 13:16-17). Receiving this mark, however, puts one on the receiving end of God's wrath.

Do you think it possible that some Christians in the tribulation period—weakened and worn down by the antichrist's relentless persecution—might be tempted to compromise their faith and receive the mark of the beast to alleviate suffering? Explain.

How might this be similar to the early Jewish Christians who sought to reduce persecution by the Jewish high priest by feigning external commitment to Judaism while secretly believing in Jesus for salvation (as indicated in the book of Hebrews)?

Why is it necessary for Christians during the tribulation period to *absolutely refuse* the mark of the beast, with no compromise?

What does Scripture reveal about the importance of *patiently enduring* through suffering, including the suffering that will result from refusing the mark of the beast?

- Matthew 10:21-22—

- Luke 21:10-19 (especially verse 19)—

- 2 Timothy 4:3-5 (especially verse 5)—

- Hebrews 10:36-39—

- Revelation 1:9—

The Antichrist Will Not Be a Muslim

Some have recently suggested that the antichrist will be a Muslim. Though the appeal of this view is understandable, it entails at least four significant problems:

1. No good Muslim would *ever* claim to be God as the antichrist will claim (read Daniel 11:36; 2 Thessalonians 2:4).

2. A Muslim antichrist claiming to be God would be viewed as an infidel among Quran-believing Muslims since Muslims believe *only Allah is God.*

3. Because Muslims believe Allah "can have no partners," they would never follow a human leader claiming to be God.

4. Islam teaches that Allah is so radically unlike any earthly reality that he cannot be described using earthly terms. How, then, could a human Muslim (the antichrist) claim to be God—a God *on earth* described *in earthly terms?*

Given current Muslim hostilities against Israel, do you think it is credible that a Muslim leader would sign a covenant with Israel guaranteeing protection for the Jews from Muslim countries?

Do you think the Jews in Israel—fully aware of Muslim animosity and hatred toward them—would ever place their hopes of survival and security entirely in the hands of a Muslim leader?

The Antichrist Will Rise in a Revived Roman Empire

Read Daniel 7:1-8. This passage refers to four beasts—representing four kingdoms—that play essential roles in biblical prophecy:

Beast One (Daniel 7:4): The imagery represents Babylon, its lion-like quality indicating power and strength.

Beast Two (Daniel 7:5): The imagery represents Medo-Persia, its bear-like qualities pointing to its strength and fierceness in battle.

Beast Three (Daniel 7:6): The imagery represents Greece under Alexander the Great. Greece's army under Alexander was leopard-like in its swiftness, cunning, and agility. The reference to the "four heads" are the four generals who divided the kingdom following Alexander's death, ruling Macedonia, Asia Minor, Syria, and Egypt.

Beast Four (Daniel 7:7-8): The mongrel imagery points to the powerful Roman Empire. This empire will be revived in the end times, comprised of ten nations ruled by ten kings. The antichrist will emerge and gain complete dominance over this revived Roman Empire.

Daniel 2 describes a prophetic dream Nebuchadnezzar had. In it, the end-time Roman Empire is pictured as a mixture of iron and clay (2:41-43). Just as iron is strong, this latter-day Roman Empire will be strong. But just as iron and clay do not naturally mix, so this latter-day Roman Empire will have some divisions. Complete internal cohesion will be lacking.

This empire will be a steppingstone for the antichrist, who will eventually gain world dominion.

With problems cascading out of control in the world today, do you think the stage is now being set for the emergence of this world leader? How?

What do you make of the tendency of many to try to identify the antichrist in the world today? Why might guessing the antichrist's identity be unwise?

Lesson from the Fig Tree

Jesus urged: "From the fig tree learn its lesson: as soon as its branch becomes tender and puts out its leaves, you know that summer is near. So also, when you see all these things, you know that he is near, at the very gates" (Matthew 24:32-33). Jesus indicates that God has revealed certain things via prophecy that ought to cause people who know the Bible to understand that a fulfillment of prophecy is taking place—or perhaps the stage is being set for a prophecy to be fulfilled. Jesus is thus informing His followers to seek to be accurate observers of the times so that when biblical prophecies are fulfilled, they will recognize it (see Luke 21:25-28).

What stage-setting do you see taking place in the world today?

If we are witnessing stage-setting for prophesied events in the tribulation period, what does that tell us about the nearness of the rapture?

DIGGING DEEPER WITH CROSS-REFERENCES

The Antichrist Mimics Christ

The antichrist will mimic the true Christ in many ways, as the following cross-references indicate:

- The true Christ performed miracles, signs, and wonders—Matthew 9:32-33; Mark 6:2.
  The antichrist will perform counterfeit miracles, signs, and wonders—Matthew 24:24; 2 Thessalonians 2:9.

- The true Christ is God—John 1:1-2; 10:31-39.
  The antichrist will claim to be God—2 Thessalonians 2:4.

- Christ's 144,000 witnesses will be sealed on their foreheads—Revelation 7:4; 14:1.
  Followers of the antichrist will be sealed on their forehead or right hand—Revelation 13:16-18.

- The true Christ will be crowned with many crowns—Revelation 19:12.
  The antichrist will be crowned with ten crowns—Revelation 13:1.

- The true Christ will ride on a white horse—Revelation 19:11.
  The antichrist will also ride on a white horse—Revelation 6:2.

- The true Christ resurrected from the dead—Matthew 28:5-10.
  The antichrist will *appear* to resurrect from the dead—Revelation 13:3, 14.

- The true Christ will have a thousand-year worldwide kingdom—Revelation 20:1-6.
  The antichrist will have a three-and-a-half-year worldwide kingdom—Revelation 13:5-8.

Dissimilarities Between Christ and the Antichrist

The following contrasts exist between Christ and the antichrist, as the following cross-references indicate:

- The true Christ causes human beings to worship God—Revelation 1:4-6.
  The antichrist will cause human beings to worship Satan—Revelation 13:3-4.

- The true Christ has a worthy name—Revelation 19:16.
  The antichrist will have blasphemous names—Revelation 13:1.

- The true Christ is called the man of sorrows—Isaiah 53:3.
  The antichrist is called the man of lawlessness—2 Thessalonians 2:3.

- The true Christ is called the Son of God—John 1:34.
  The antichrist is called the son of destruction—2 Thessalonians 2:3.

- The true Christ is called the Lamb—Isaiah 53:7.
  The antichrist is called the beast—Revelation 11:7.

- The true Christ is called the Holy One of God—Mark 1:24.
  The antichrist is called the lawless one—2 Thessalonians 2:8.

- The true Christ came to do the Father's will—John 6:38.
  The antichrist will do his own will—Daniel 11:36.

- The true Christ was energized by the Holy Spirit—Luke 4:14.
  The antichrist will be energized by Satan, the unholy spirit—Revelation 13:4.

- The true Christ submitted Himself to God—John 5:30.
  The antichrist will defy God—2 Thessalonians 2:4.

- The true Christ humbled Himself—Philippians 2:8.
  The antichrist will exalt himself—Daniel 11:37.

- The true Christ cleansed the temple—John 2:13-17.
  The antichrist will defile the temple—Matthew 24:15.

- The true Christ was slain for the people—John 11:51.
  The antichrist will slay the people—Isaiah 14:20.

- The true Christ was received up into heaven—Luke 24:51.
  The antichrist will go down into the lake of fire—Revelation 19:20.

PRAYER

Father, even today we witness the stage being set for multiple prophecies to be fulfilled in the not-too-distant future. This makes me think that maybe the day of the rapture is drawing near. That possibility motivates me to be ready by living the way You want me to live. Every day that passes brings me one day closer to when Jesus is coming for me. It is a wondrous thing to think about. Thank You in Jesus's name. Amen.

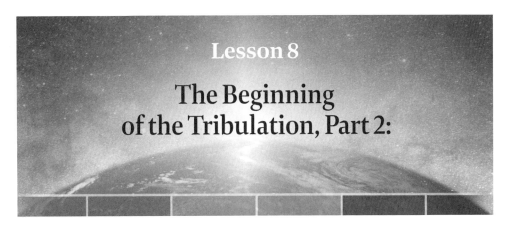

Lesson 8

The Beginning of the Tribulation, Part 2:

Rebuilt Temple and Signs of the End

◼ KEY CONCEPT

The Jewish temple will be rebuilt in the early part of the tribulation period. Concurrently, prophetic signs of the times will indicate that the end times are now in full swing.

◼ THE BIG IDEAS IN THIS LESSON

- The Jewish temple will be rebuilt in the early part of the tribulation period. Temple sacrifices will be reinstated—but only for the first three-and-a-half years of the tribulation. The antichrist will desecrate the temple at the midpoint of the tribulation. He will then prevent any further sacrifices in the temple.

- Prophetic signs of the times will concurrently indicate that the end times are now in full swing. There will be *earth and sky signs* (cosmic disturbances such as earthquakes and signs in the heavens), *moral signs* (immorality will escalate dramatically), *religious signs* (false Christs and false prophets will proliferate), and *technological signs* (various technologies will facilitate globalism, economic control, and the potential for global destruction).

◼ PROBING THE SCRIPTURES

The Jewish Temple Will Be Rebuilt

The temple has long played a prominent role among the Jewish people. There have been three temples so far. Solomon built the first one, and it became the heart and center of Jewish worship (1 Kings 6–7; 2 Chronicles 3–4). The Jews continually disobeyed God, however, and—as a disciplinary measure—God sent them into exile at the hands of the Babylonians, who destroyed Solomon's temple in 587 BC.

What do we learn about God's discipline in the following Bible passages?

- Hebrews 12:5-11—

- Proverbs 3:11-12—

- Job 5:17—

- Psalm 118:18—

- Psalm 119:75—

Following the Babylonian exile, many Jews returned to Jerusalem and constructed a smaller version of Solomon's temple. It was a dim reflection of the original, but lasted a good five hundred years.

Israel's third temple in Jerusalem was built by King Herod the Great. It was completed in AD 64. Although enormous and magnificent, it was destroyed in AD 70 (along with the rest of Jerusalem) by Titus and his Roman warriors.

The Coming Tribulation Temple

As noted previously, yet another temple will be built early in the tribulation period. Animal sacrifices will be reinstated. However, the antichrist will cause these sacrifices to cease at the midpoint of the tribulation (Daniel 9:27). From henceforth, he will set himself up as the world's only object of worship as "God on earth" (2 Thessalonians 2:4; Revelation 13:5-8).

Though the temple does not need to be rebuilt until the tribulation period, preparations are in the works *even now* for its rebuilding:

- The Jewish Sanhedrin has been reestablished. This is significant because the Sanhedrin will choose the high priest for the coming temple.

- The Jewish Sanhedrin is currently raising money for the rebuilding of the temple.

- The Jewish Sanhedrin has hired architects to design plans for the rebuilding of the temple.

- Priestly robes, temple tapestries, worship utensils, and other items are now being prefabricated so that when the temple is finally rebuilt, everything will be ready for it.

If plans are being made *even now* to build the tribulation temple, what implications does this have for the nearness of the rapture? Explain.

In view of the apparent nearness of the rapture, is there any moral cleanup you need to do in your life? Explain.

Signs of the Times

A "sign of the times" is an event of prophetic significance that points to the end times. We might say that these signs constitute God's *intel in advance* regarding what the world will look like as we enter the end times.

Toward the end of Jesus's ministry on earth, the disciples asked Him specifically about the tribulation period: "Tell us, when will these things be, and what will be the sign of your coming and of the end of the age?" (Matthew 24:3). Jesus then spoke of specific signs of the times that will emerge and intensify in the years before the second coming—that is, during the tribulation period (24:4-28).

Christians should take these signs of the times seriously. Recall that Jesus chastised the Jewish leaders for ignoring the "signs of the times" related to His first coming. Both the Sadducees and the Pharisees were blind to the signs that pointed to His identity as the divine Messiah.

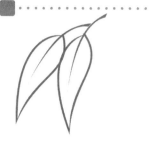

Read Matthew 16:1-3. How did Jesus describe the Jewish leaders' blindness to the signs of the times?

Jesus referred to some of the signs of His divine Messiahship in Matthew 11:1-6. What are they?

How do the signs of the times Jesus mentioned in Matthew 11:1-6 correlate with the messianic prophecies in Isaiah 35:5-6?

How do the miraculous works of Jesus in Matthew 15:29-31 correlate with the messianic prophecies in Isaiah 35:5-6?

Were some of the Jewish leaders aware that Jesus performed the sign of healing the blind (John 9:13-17)?

Were the Jewish leaders aware that Jesus healed the lame (Luke 5:17-26)?

Why do you think the Jewish leaders were hardened against Jesus, despite these clear signs that proved His identity as the divine Messiah?

Here is the important lesson we learn from all this: You and I are called by Jesus to be thoughtful observers of the times. We are to be aware of what biblical prophecy teaches and then keep a close eye on unfolding events in the world so that we become aware of any possible correlation between world events and biblical prophecy. It is

wise to sharpen our abilities to see the significance of the signs of the times. Let us not harden ourselves against prophetic signs, as did the ancient Jews.

Don't Set Dates

Even though we are to watch for the signs of the times, we should also be careful to avoid setting dates for the future fulfillment of Bible prophecies.

What does Matthew 24:36 tell us about this?

What does Acts 1:6-7 tell us about this?

Even though we shouldn't set dates, we can still confidently rejoice that we are living in the *general season* of the Lord's return.

What does Matthew 24:32-33 tell us about this?

Since the signs of the times can give us clues that we are in the general season of the Lord's return, it makes good sense to understand some of these signs. There are four categories: earth and sky signs, moral signs, religious signs, and technological signs.

Earth and Sky Signs

There will be a significant increase in frequency and intensity of earthquakes, famine, pestilence, and signs in the heavens in the future tribulation period.

What do you learn about this from Matthew 24:7-8?

Why do you think the events described in these verses are called "the beginning of the birth pains"?

Summarize the earth and sky signs described in Luke 21:11:

What do you think is meant by "terrors and great signs from heaven"?

An insight from the Greek: The term *terrors* carries the idea "sights of terror" or "terrifying things."

Does Revelation 8:10-11 help you to understand what might be meant by "terrors and great signs from heaven"?

Many believe this "star" will involve near-extinction-level deep impact of a giant meteor or an asteroid striking planet Earth. It has the appearance of a star because it bursts into flames—burning like a torch—as it plummets through earth's atmosphere. It turns a third of the waters on earth bitter so that people who drink it die. It may contaminate this large volume of water by the residue that results from the meteor disintegrating as it blasts through the earth's atmosphere. Or it may be that the meteor plummets into the headwaters from which some of the world's major rivers and underground water sources flow, thereby spreading the contaminated water to many people on earth.

Read Revelation 8:12. Do you think it possible that a deep impact of a large meteor might kick up dust into the atmosphere and cause a reduction in sunlight and other celestial bodies? Why or why not?

Some have also suggested that the "terrors and great signs from heaven" might include appearances of UFOs in the sky.

Do you agree with this idea? Why or why not?

Some prophecy enthusiasts suggest that alleged aliens and UFOs might be part of the "strong delusion" God will send upon the world in judgment (2 Thessalonians 2:11). Do you agree or disagree with this idea? Why?

Moral Signs

Prophetic Scripture speaks of moral signs that will escalate during the future tribulation period.

Read 2 Timothy 3:1-5 and list some of the signs of moral degradation of the last days:

Three Modern Philosophies

- "Lovers of self" (2 Timothy 3:2) is a biblical way of describing *humanism*.
- "Lovers of money" (2 Timothy 3:2) is a biblical way of describing *materialism*.
- "Lovers of pleasure" (2 Timothy 3:4) is a biblical way of describing *hedonism*.

Summarize how these three philosophies have become increasingly prominent in our own day. Be specific.

These days, it seems that people are far more interested in *happiness* than in *holiness*. They yearn more for *pleasure* than for *praising God*. Humanism, materialism, and hedonism will reign supreme in the end times!

> What does Jesus say about moral degradation in Matthew 24:12, 37-39?
>
>
>
> While Jesus's words have specific reference to the future tribulation period, do you notice the days-of-Noah attitude even in our day? How so?

Religious Signs

There are many religious signs associated with the tribulation period. For example, there will be a notable increase of false christs and false prophets. A counterfeit christ or counterfeit prophet who preaches a counterfeit gospel will yield a counterfeit salvation (see Galatians 1:8). There are no exceptions to this maxim. From a religious perspective, this is one thing that makes the tribulation period so deceptive and dangerous.

Even in our day, we witness an unprecedented rise in false christs and false prophets affiliated with the kingdom of the cults and the occult. This will escalate dramatically as we move deeper into the end times.

> What does Jesus say about false christs and false prophets in Matthew 24:23-24?
>
>
> What do you think about the possibility of "the elect" being led astray?
>
>
> What do you learn about false prophets from Matthew 7:15-20?

Can you think of any false prophets in the world today? What makes them false?

How are false christs and false prophets setting the stage for the ultimate false christ (the antichrist) and the ultimate false prophet in the tribulation period? Be specific.

Another religious sign of the end times relates to the increase of apostasy: What does 1 Timothy 4:1 tell us about apostasy in the end times?

What does 2 Timothy 4:3-4 tell us about apostasy in the end times?

Do you think we are witnessing such things in our day? How so?

What can you do to insulate yourself against the rising apostasy in our world? How do the Berean Christians set a good example for us (Acts 17:11)?

Technological Signs

Some of the events prophesied of the tribulation period require technological advances to make them possible. We might call these technological signs. Many prophecy scholars believe the technology is now in place for these various prophecies to be fulfilled.

Read Matthew 24:14. What kinds of technology might be necessary to accomplish complete global evangelism?

Read Revelation 13:16-17 for a summary of the false prophet's enforcement of the mark of the beast as related to the control of the global economy. What kinds of technology might be necessary to enforce the mark of the beast?

Read Revelation 8:7. The fire described here could be directly inflicted by God, or it could be man-made. What kind of technology might be necessary to burn up a third of the earth?

Read Revelation 16:2. Do you think it is possible that the same technology that can burn up a third of the earth can also cause painful sores to come upon people? How so?

Read Luke 21:25-26. Some prophecy experts suggest Jesus may be referring to nuclear weaponry when He says, "The powers of the heavens will be shaken." Do you agree or disagree? Why?

Having briefly surveyed earth and sky signs, moral signs, religious signs, and technological signs that will predominate during the tribulation period, we can observe that these prophetic signs are now casting their shadows before them. They are emerging in preliminary form in our day. We can logically infer that the stage is being set for the tribulation period.

Has your study of biblical prophecy bolstered your faith in God and your confidence in the Bible? If so, how?

Knowing that the rapture could occur at any time, are you more motivated to walk in righteousness before the Lord?

LIFE LESSONS

The Danger of Misplaced Love

Many people who live during the future tribulation period will be "lovers of self," "lovers of money," and "lovers of pleasure." Second Corinthians 13:5 urges, "Examine yourselves, to see whether you are in the faith. Test yourselves." Here is a worthy exercise: *Examine yourself for any traces of misplaced love.* Are there any midcourse adjustments you need to make in your life?

The Danger of Misplaced Worship

Many people in the tribulation period will worship the antichrist (2 Thessalonians 2:4; Revelation 13:8). Scripture reveals, however, that *God alone* is to be worshipped (Matthew 4:10; Acts 14:11-18; Revelation 19:10). Worship involves reverencing God, adoring Him, praising Him, venerating Him, and paying homage to Him, not just outwardly in a corporate setting but in our hearts as well. Even the way we live our lives can be a worshipful act (see Romans 12:1).

DIGGING DEEPER WITH CROSS-REFERENCES

Recognizing a False Prophet

False prophets give false prophecies—Deuteronomy 18:21-22.
They promote false gods or idols—Exodus 20:3-4; Deuteronomy 13:1-3.
They often deny the deity of Christ—Colossians 2:8-9.
They sometimes deny Christ's humanity—1 John 4:1-3.
They often promote immorality—Jude 4-7.

They often encourage legalistic self-denial—Colossians 2:16-23.

Three Key Denials of Apostates

Denial of God—2 Timothy 3:1-5.

Denial of Christ—1 John 2:18-22.

Denial of the Faith—1 Timothy 4:1-2; 2 Timothy 4:3-4.

PRAYER

Father, I am awed that You are sovereignly guiding human history toward its culmination. You are in control. Nothing can happen that is outside the scope of Your divine authority. Though some aspects of Bible prophecy seem frightening, You have instructed us to trust You (John 14:1-3), to walk closely with You (Proverbs 3:5-6), and to rejoice in the awe-inspiring future that awaits us in heaven (Revelation 21–22). Please grant us the enabling grace to live in a way that pleases You in these end times. I pray in Jesus's name. Amen.

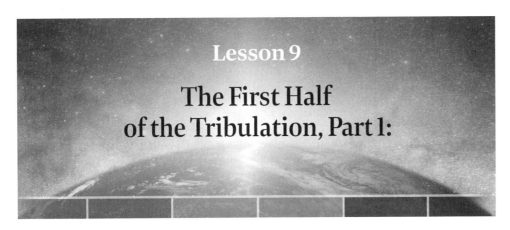

Lesson 9

The First Half of the Tribulation, Part 1:

The Lamb and His Witnesses

■ KEY CONCEPT

Early in the tribulation period, Jesus in heaven will receive a seven-sealed scroll. Meanwhile on earth, Christ's servants—the 144,000 Jewish evangelists and the two prophetic witnesses—will begin their ministries.

■ THE BIG IDEAS IN THIS LESSON

- Early in the tribulation period, Jesus "the Lamb" will receive a seven-sealed scroll. He will be the only one worthy in heaven to receive it. He will soon open the seals of the scroll one by one, with each bringing a terrible judgment upon the unbelieving world.

- Meanwhile, on earth, the 144,000 Jewish evangelists will begin their ministry around the world, preaching the gospel of the kingdom. Their work will yield a mighty harvest of souls.

- God's two prophetic witnesses will also engage in ministry during this time. The power of these witnesses is like that of Elijah and Moses. They will bear witness to the truth.

■ PROBING THE SCRIPTURES

The Lamb Will Receive the Seven-Sealed Scroll

Read Revelation 5. In what specific ways is this entire scene Christ-exalting?

Christ is referred to as both a lamb and a lion.

- Christ was a *lamb* at His first coming. He shed His blood for the sins of humankind as the Lamb of God.

- Christ will be a *lion* at the second coming. Instead of coming again in meekness, He will come with great strength and fierceness.

This lamb—who is also a lion—is *all-powerful*, having "seven horns." A horn on an animal was used by that animal as a weapon (Genesis 22:13; Psalm 69:31). For this reason, the horn eventually came to represent power and might. As an extension of this symbol, horns were also seen as emblems of dominion, representing kingdoms and kings, as in the books of Daniel and Revelation (Daniel 7–8; Revelation 12:3; 13:1, 11; 17:3-16).

Here's the critical thing to remember: The number seven in the Bible indicates "completeness" or "perfection." That Christ has seven horns points to His *complete and perfect dominion and omnipotence.* He is all-powerful. That Christ has seven eyes likewise means He *sees all and is all-knowing.*

Can you think of examples anywhere in Scripture where Christ's omnipotence is evident?

How do the following Bible passages point to Christ's omnipotence?

- Colossians 1:16-17—

- Hebrews 1:3—

- Matthew 8:23-27—

- John 11:38-44—

- Revelation 19:11-16—

Revelation 5:6 refers to "the seven spirits of God sent out into all the earth." Many Bible expositors believe this is a reference to the Holy Spirit (Revelation 1:4; 4:5). There are two reasons:

1. Isaiah 11:2 refers to *seven aspects* of the Spirit of the Lord.

2. Seven is the number of "completeness" or "perfection." Used of the Holy Spirit, this number may represent the perfection of the Holy Spirit, and the perfection and completeness of His work.

What do you learn about some of the perfect works of the Holy Spirit in the following Bible passages?

- Galatians 5:22-23—

- 2 Peter 1:21—

- Romans 8:26—

- Titus 3:4-7—

- John 15:26—

- John 16:13—

- Ephesians 4:30—

Can you write a one-sentence summary of the perfect work of the Holy Spirit as reflected in these verses?

Because Christ—the lamb/lion—was found worthy, He "took the scroll from the right hand of him who was seated on the throne" (Revelation 5:7). This reminds us of a prophecy recorded by Daniel in Old Testament times.

Read Daniel 7:13-14. Take a few moments to ponder these heavenly scenes involving the Father and the Son, the first and second persons of the Trinity.

- What do you learn about the Father in Revelation 5:7 and Daniel 7:13-14?

- What do you learn about the Son in Revelation 5:7 and Daniel 7:13-14?

After the lamb/lion takes the scroll from the Father, the twenty-four elders will fall down and worship Jesus (Revelation 5:8). This is as it should be, for Christ—*as*

God—has always been worshipped, even during His time on earth. He always accepted such worship as appropriate.

Briefly summarize the worship of Jesus in the following passages:

- Hebrews 1:6—

- Matthew 2:7-11—

- Matthew 14:28-33—

- John 9:35-38—

- Matthew 28:1-9—

- Luke 24:50-53—

Why not take a few moments and worship the Lord Jesus right now?

Read the lyrics of the "new song" in Revelation 5:9-10. Can you think of any answers to prayer or spiritual experiences with God that move you to exult, "Worthy are You, O Lord"? Talk to the Lord about it right now!

This wondrous scene in heaven chronologically sets the stage for all that follows, for soon we will witness the lamb/lion opening the seven seals. As each respective seal is opened, a judgment—expressing God's wrath—will fall upon the world.

The 144,000 Jewish Evangelists Will Engage in Ministry

Read Revelation 7:4.

Some Bible interpreters claim this verse might be a metaphorical reference to the Christian church. However, the very fact that specific tribes are mentioned in this context, along with specific numbers for those tribes (twelve), removes all possibility that this is a metaphor or figure of speech. Nowhere else in the Bible does a reference to the twelve tribes of Israel mean anything but the twelve tribes of Israel. Indeed, the word *tribe* is never used of anything but a literal ethnic group in Scripture.

- *Eisegesis* involves reading a meaning into the text that is not there.

- *Exegesis* involves deriving the meaning from the text itself.

Why is it especially bad to use eisegesis in interpreting Bible prophecy? Be specific.

Chapters 2 and 3 in the book of Revelation speak of the seven churches of Asia Minor. The word *church* is sprinkled throughout these chapters. Chapters 4–18, which speak of the tribulation period, do not mention *church* a single time. Why? Because the church is not in the tribulation period.

I remind you of this interpretive principle: *When the plain sense makes good sense, seek no other sense lest you end up in nonsense.*

It does not make good sense to say that "the twelve tribes of Israel" refers to the church. It makes perfect sense to take this as referring to twelve literal tribes of Israel. The church will have already been removed from the earth at the rapture.

If the church is raptured *before* the tribulation period, how could Revelation 7:4 (the "144,000, sealed from every tribe of the sons of Israel") refer to the church?

Here is my take: The backdrop to a proper understanding of the 144,000 during the tribulation is that *God initially chose the Jews to be His witnesses.* Their appointed task was to share the good news of God with all other people around the world (Isaiah 42:6; 43:10). The Jews were to be God's representatives to the Gentile peoples.

Biblical history reveals that the Jews failed at this task. They didn't even recognize Jesus as the divine Messiah. Nevertheless, this was their calling.

During the future tribulation period, these 144,000 Jews—who become believers in Jesus sometime following the rapture—will finally fulfill this mandate from God. They will be His evangelists all around the world. Their work will yield a mighty harvest of souls (Revelation 7:9-14).

These evangelists will be protectively sealed by God. They will be divinely protected as they carry out their service for God on the earth during the tribulation (Revelation 14:1-4).

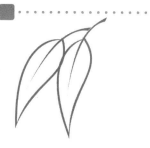

They will emerge in the early part of the tribulation period, sometime after the rapture. We know this because Scripture prophesies that many believers will be martyred in the first half of the tribulation period (Revelation 6:9-11). Where will these many believers come from? It seems likely that they will be converted *after being evangelized* by the 144,000 Jewish evangelists!

This may be a hard question for some: If it ever came to it, do you think you would give your life as a martyr instead of denying Jesus Christ at gunpoint?

The persecution of God's people will be widespread during the tribulation period. Can you think of a time when someone persecuted you, mocked you, or spoke condescendingly of you for being a Christian? How did you respond?

Many wonder: How will these 144,000 Jews convert to Christ during the tribulation period? To answer this question, read about Saul's conversion experience in Acts 9:1-9. Then read 1 Corinthians 15:8.

Why do you think Paul referred to himself as "one untimely born"?

I think it is possible that the 144,000 Jews will become believers in Jesus in a way similar to that of Paul, himself a Jew. When Paul refers to himself as "one untimely born," he may have been alluding to his 144,000 Jewish tribulation brethren. Perhaps they will be spiritually born in a way similar to him—only Paul was spiritually born *far before* they were (in an *untimely* way). Just as Paul was supernaturally born again through a direct encounter with the risen Jesus, so the 144,000 Jewish brethren may likewise become born again through a direct encounter with the risen Jesus.

Do the 144,000 Jewish evangelists who fearlessly proclaim the gospel of the kingdom motivate you to be a better witness for Christ in your circle of influence?

God's Two Prophetic Witnesses Will Engage in Ministry

In addition to the 144,000 Jewish witnesses, God will also raise up two mighty prophetic witnesses to testify to the true God with incredible power during the tribulation period. The power of these two witnesses recalls Elijah (1 Kings 17; Malachi 4:5) and Moses (Exodus 7–11). In the Old Testament, two witnesses were required to confirm testimony (Deuteronomy 17:6; 19:15; Matthew 18:16; John 8:17; Hebrews 10:28).

Read Revelation 11:3-6. Summarize the incredible miraculous powers of these two witnesses.

Why will such miraculous powers be necessary during the tribulation period?

Some suggest the following evidence that these prophetic witnesses may indeed be Moses and Elijah:

- In the tribulation period (the seventieth week of Daniel), God will deal heavily with the Jews—just as He did in the first sixty-nine weeks of Daniel (Daniel 9:24-27). Since Moses and Elijah are the two most influential figures in Jewish history, it makes good sense that they will be on the scene during the tribulation.

- Moses and Elijah appeared on the mount of transfiguration with Jesus (Matthew 17:1-8). This shows their centrality.

- The miracles portrayed in Revelation 11 are like those previously performed by Moses and Elijah in Old Testament times.

What is your view? Will Moses and Elijah reappear during the tribulation period? Or will God raise up two entirely new prophets with similar powers? Provide reasons for your view.

The time frame for these two witnesses is 1260 days, which measures out to precisely three-and-a-half years—half of the tribulation period. Most prophecy scholars believe the two witnesses will do their miraculous work during the first half of the tribulation period.

After they finish their assigned work from God, they will be executed at the midpoint of the tribulation period. Soon after, God will resurrect them from the dead.

Read about this in Revelation 11:7-12.

How will the resurrection of the two witnesses be a powerful attestation of the truth of all they taught during their ministry?

After having had a Christmas party following the execution of the two witnesses, what do you think the response of onlookers will be when the two witnesses are resurrected?

Why do you think people will still refuse to turn to Christ for salvation after witnessing such divine power?

LIFE LESSONS

God Seals His People

Just as the 144,000 Jewish believers received God's seal, so believers today are sealed by the Holy Spirit. Ephesians 1:13-14 tells us that we "were sealed with the promised Holy Spirit, who is the guarantee of our inheritance until we acquire possession of it, to the praise of his glory." This is why we are exhorted: "Do not grieve the Holy Spirit of God, by whom you were sealed for the day of redemption" (Ephesians 4:30). Because our salvation is secure (it is "sealed"), we can now live in joyful thanks every day (Psalm 100; Philippians 4:4-7).

God and Judgment

While God is a God of love, grace, and mercy, He is also a God of judgment in the face of unrepentant sin. Judgment fell upon the Jews for rejecting Christ (Matthew 21:43), on Ananias and Sapphira for lying to God (Acts 5), on Herod for self-exalting pride (Acts 12:21-23), and on Christians in Corinth for irreverence during the Lord's Supper (1 Corinthians 11:27-32; 1 John 5:16). Christians will stand before the judgment seat of Christ (1 Corinthians 3:12-15; 2 Corinthians 5:10). Unbelievers will face the great white throne judgment (Revelation 20:11-15). *No one is getting away with anything.*

DIGGING DEEPER WITH CROSS-REFERENCES

The Lamb of God

The Lamb's blood—Revelation 12:11.
The Lamb takes away the sins of the world—John 1:29.
The Lamb is victorious—Revelation 17:14.
The Lamb stands before the throne—Revelation 7:17.
The Lamb's wrath—Revelation 6:15-17.
The Lamb's book of life—Revelation 21:27.
The Lamb lights up the eternal city—Revelation 21:23.

Worship

Worship and bow down—Psalm 95:6.
Worship the Creator—Revelation 14:7.
Worship with reverence—Hebrews 12:28-29.
Worship in spirit and truth—John 4:20-24.
Worship the only true God—Exodus 20:3-5; Deuteronomy 5:7; Matthew 4:10.
Worship the Lord with gladness—Psalm 29:2; 100:1-2.

PRAYER ·

Worthy are You, our Lord and God, to receive glory and honor and power, for You created all things, and by Your will, they existed and were created. You alone are worthy of worship. May Your Word motivate my heart to center on You as the sole object of worship in my life. Let there be no idols. Let there be no competitors on the throne of my heart. You alone are worthy. I pray in Jesus's name. Amen.

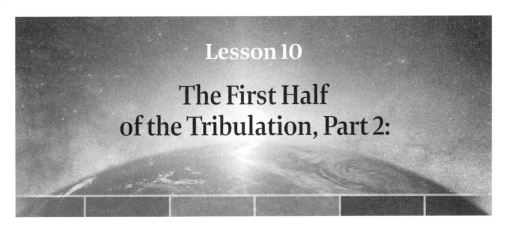

Lesson 10

The First Half of the Tribulation, Part 2:

Judgments, Martyrdom, and Apostasy

■ KEY CONCEPT

Unimaginably hard times will fall upon those living during the tribulation period. God's judgments will fall. Many of God's people will be martyred. A global false religion will emerge and deceive multitudes.

■ THE BIG IDEAS IN THIS LESSON

- The seal judgments will be unleashed upon the earth.

- God's people will increasingly suffer martyrdom. Satan and the antichrist will both target believers.

- Things will go from bad to worse when the trumpet judgments are unleashed upon the earth.

- The false religion associated with New Babylon will emerge into global dominance. This apostate religion will seem outwardly glorious while being inwardly corrupt, will deceive multitudes of people, will exercise powerful political clout, and will persecute God's people during the tribulation period.

■ PROBING THE SCRIPTURES

The word *tribulation* literally means "to press hard upon" or "to be hard pressed," and refers to times of oppression, affliction, and distress. The Greek word (*thlipsis*) is translated variously as "tribulation," "affliction," "anguish," "persecution," "trouble," and "burden."

This word has been used in relation to those hard-pressed by the calamities of war (Matthew 24:21), a woman giving birth to a child (John 16:21), the afflictions of

Christ (Colossians 1:24), those pressed by poverty and lack (Philippians 4:14), great anxiety and burden of the heart (2 Corinthians 2:4), and a period in the end times that will have unparalleled tribulation (Revelation 7:14).

What does Jesus teach about the general tribulation we all face (John 16:33)?

What does the apostle Paul teach about the general tribulation we all face (Acts 14:21-22)?

What does Philippians 4:6-7 say we can experience when we entrust our problems to God?

Are there any forms of tribulation now pressing on you that you would like to entrust to God's care? List them here.

Though we all experience *general* tribulation in day-to-day living, this is distinct from the *specific* "tribulation period" of the end times. The following scriptural facts make this clear:

- Scripture refers to a definite period of tribulation at the end of the age (Matthew 24:29-35).

- This period will be so severe that no period in history—past or future— will equal it (Matthew 24:21).

- This period will be shortened for the elect's sake (Matthew 24:22), for no human being would survive otherwise.

- It is called "a time of distress for Jacob" because Messiah-rejecting Israel will experience God's judgment during this period (Jeremiah 30:7; Daniel 12:1-4).

- The unbelieving nations will also be judged for their sin and rejection of Jesus Christ (Isaiah 26:21; Revelation 6:15-17).

- The tribulation period will last seven years (Daniel 9:24, 27).

- Things will be so bad that people will want to hide and even die (Revelation 6:16).

- This period features three sets of God's judgments—the seal judgments, the trumpet judgments, and the bowl judgments. These increasingly worse judgments will be expressions of God's wrath.

This period will be unimaginably bad. Scripture assures us that this period will be characterized by wrath (Zephaniah 1:15-18), judgment (Revelation 14:7), indignation (Isaiah 26:20-21), trial (Revelation 3:10), trouble (Jeremiah 30:7), destruction (Joel 1:15), darkness (Amos 5:18-20), desolation (Daniel 9:27), overturning (Isaiah 24:1-4), and punishment (Isaiah 24:20-21).

You *won't* want to be there. The good news is that Scripture promises that the church will be removed prior to the beginning of the tribulation period:

Quick Review: Summarize the wonderful promises in…

- 1 Thessalonians 1:9-10—

- 1 Thessalonians 5:9-10—

- Revelation 3:10—

- Romans 5:9—

The Seven Seal Judgments Will Be Unleashed

Human suffering will steadily escalate during the tribulation period. The first set of divine judgments to be unleashed on the earth are the seal judgments.

Summarize what happens in each of the following judgments:

- First seal judgment (Revelation 6:1-2)—

- Second seal judgment (Revelation 6:3-4)—

- Third seal judgment (Revelation 6:5-6)—

- Fourth seal judgment (Revelation 6:7-8)—

- Fifth seal judgment (Revelation 6:9-11)—

- Sixth seal judgment (Revelation 6:12-17)—

The seventh seal judgment will bring on an entirely new set of judgments called the trumpet judgments (Revelation 8). We will examine these shortly.

Parallels to Jesus's Olivet Discourse

Jesus gave a prophetic sermon called the Olivet Discourse, so-named because He was sitting on the Mount of Olives when He delivered the discourse (Matthew 24–25). A good portion of this sermon deals with what will transpire during the tribulation period. Some of Jesus's prophecies find direct parallels with some of the seal judgments in Revelation.

Consult the following verses and jot down the parallels:

Antichrist/false christs

- The first seal judgment (Revelation 6:1-2)—

- Jesus's prophecy (Matthew 24:4-5)—

No peace/war

- The second seal judgment (Revelation 6:3-4)—

- Jesus's prophecy (Matthew 24:6)—

Hard to buy food/famine

- The third seal judgment (Revelation 6:5-6)—

- Jesus's prophecy (Matthew 24:7)—

Earthquakes

- The sixth seal judgment (Revelation 6:12-14)—

- Jesus's prophecy (Matthew 24:7)—

What do you think is the significance of such similarities?

Martyrdom Will Escalate

The church will be raptured prior to the tribulation period (1 Thessalonians 1:9-10; 4:13-17; 5:9; Revelation 3:10). Many other people, however, will become believers during the tribulation (Matthew 25:31-46). There will be a "great multitude" of conversions (Revelation 7:9-10).

While many of these believers in Jesus will still be alive by the time of Christ's second coming (following the tribulation period), many others will be martyred on earth during the tribulation.

What do you learn about some of these martyrs in Revelation 6:9-11?

How does this passage indicate there are more martyrs to come?

How do we know that believers who die are now in a better state? To answer this question, summarize the following verses:

- 2 Corinthians 5:8—

- Philippians 1:21-24—

- Psalm 16:11—

God's people will be persecuted during the tribulation period. Some of them will be martyred. But death for them will simply be a *gateway into life*—eternal life with Jesus, the divine Messiah.

The Trumpet Judgments Will Be Unleashed

The seal judgments, as bad as they are, are followed by even worse judgments—*the trumpet judgments* (Revelation 8). Things go from bad to worse in the tribulation period.

Summarize what happens in each of the following judgments:

- First trumpet judgment (Revelation 8:7)—

- Second trumpet judgment (Revelation 8:8-9)—

- Third trumpet judgment (Revelation 8:10-11)—

- Fourth trumpet judgment (Revelation 8:12-13)—

- Fifth trumpet judgment (Revelation 9:1-12)—

- Sixth trumpet judgment (Revelation 9:13-21)—

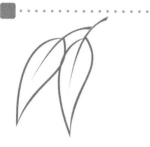

Do you think the fire that falls on the earth in the first trumpet judgment might involve nuclear weaponry? Or does the fire come directly from God?

Is it possible that the "star" that falls from heaven in the third trumpet judgment is a large meteor or asteroid that makes deep impact on the earth? If so, why do you think it is described as a star?

Is it possible that the darkness of the sun, moon, and stars might be due to dust kicking up into the atmosphere after a giant asteroid associated with the third trumpet judgment strikes the earth? Or will the darkness be directly inflicted by God?

How might the darkened sun increase the level of famine on earth? (Think in terms of plant life.)

Do you see a domino effect in some of these judgments, with one leading to another? Explain.

What would you say to an atheist who claims a loving God would never allow plagues to kill a third of humankind, as described in the sixth trumpet judgment?

The seventh trumpet will initiate a new set of judgments called the bowl judgments. These are even worse than the trumpet judgments (Revelation 16). Woe to those on the earth at this time.

Do prophecies like those we have explored in this lesson make you stressful?

How can you maintain a sense of peace (Isaiah 26:3; John 14:1, 27; Philippians 4:6-7)?

Religious Babylon Will Dominate the World

Revelation 17 speaks of the nature and influence of religious Babylon:

- Verses 1-7 provide a description of it.

- Verses 8-18 provide an interpretation of it.

- Throughout, there is much symbolic language.

- Religious Babylon is labeled *a great prostitute*—a graphic metaphor symbolizing unfaithfulness to God, idolatry, and religious apostasy (Jeremiah 3:6-10; Ezekiel 20:30-31; Hosea 4:7-15; 5:3-4; 6:10; 9:1).

The falsehoods of religious Babylon will influence the people of many nations (Revelation 17:1). The kings and rulers of the world—even the antichrist—will fall within the grips of this false religious system (Revelation 14:8). It will emerge into prominence during the first half of the tribulation period.

Revelation 17 reveals that this apostate religious system…

- will be worldwide in its impact (verse 15).

- will seem outwardly glorious while being inwardly corrupt (implied in verse 4).

- will persecute true believers during the tribulation period (verse 6).

Do you think the stage is now being set for the emergence of this false religious system? How so?

What kind of apostasy are we witnessing even now within Christian churches? Be specific.

Does false doctrine bother you when you encounter it? Do you ever feel tempted to turn a blind eye toward it to avoid conflict with others?

Why do you think both Jesus and the apostle Paul went to such great lengths to warn Christians against deception (Matthew 7:15-20; 24:4-5, 11; Galatians 1:6-9; 2 Corinthians 11:3-4)? Did they believe Christians are vulnerable to deception? *Do you think you are vulnerable to deception?*

How does Scripture knowledge insulate us from apostasy and false doctrine?

- 2 Timothy 3:16—

- Acts 17:11—

- Romans 12:2—

- 1 Thessalonians 5:20-21—

- Psalm 119:9-11—

Trusting God's Control over the Prophetic Future

One of the purposes of Bible prophecy is to bring comfort to God's people. The book of Revelation is a good example. The recipients of this book were suffering persecution, and some were even being martyred (Revelation 2:13). John wrote this book to give his readers a strong hope that would help them patiently endure relentless suffering (Revelation 21–22). John urged them to persist in trusting God.

We see the same thing in the book of Daniel. The Jewish captivity in Babylon was not the end of the story (Daniel 1:1-4). Daniel knew deliverance was coming. Meanwhile, patient endurance during captivity was the need of the day.

In a world that often seems out of control, we too can trust that God will intervene, overcome evil, and bring deliverance to us. We are instructed to trust God at all times (Psalm 62:8), and especially in times of trouble (Psalm 50:15). We are exhorted to trust God with a whole heart (Proverbs 3:5-6), knowing that He is all-too-willing to help us (Psalm 37:5). All who trust in the Lord will rejoice (Psalm 5:11-12; 40:4).

Babylon Versus Jerusalem

- While Jerusalem means "city of peace," Babylon means "city of confusion and war." They are antithetical to each other.

- While Jerusalem is portrayed as God's city in the Bible (Revelation 21:2-3), Babylon is described as a demonic city (18:2).

- While God's temple was built (and will one day be rebuilt) in Jerusalem, the Tower of Babel was built in Babylon (Genesis 11:1-9).

- The book of Revelation describes the New Jerusalem as a chaste bride (Revelation 21:9-10). New Babylon is described as a great prostitute (17:1-6).

- While the New Jerusalem is portrayed as an eternal city (Revelation 21:1-4), New Babylon is described as a temporal city that will be destroyed by God toward the end of the seven-year tribulation period (18:8).

- As Christians, the good news is that you and I will live in the New Jerusalem for all eternity. John 14:1-3 tells us that Jesus Himself is building this heavenly eternal city for us. All our Christian loved ones will be there, so there will be some great reunions in this city.

Persecution

All the godly suffer persecution—2 Timothy 3:12.

Blessed are those persecuted for righteousness—Matthew 5:10-12.

A brother will betray brother—Matthew 10:21-22.

Don't be surprised if the world hates you—1 John 3:13.

God blesses those mocked for following Jesus—Luke 6:22-23.

Moses chose affliction over the pleasures of sin—Hebrews 11:24-25.

Paul was beaten, jailed, and mobbed—2 Corinthians 6:3-5.

Persecution broke out after Stephen's death—Acts 11:19.

Pray for those who persecute you—Matthew 5:44.

Rejoice in being counted worthy to suffer—Acts 5:41.

Suffering for doing good—1 Peter 3:17.

Suffer with Christ now; be glorified with Christ later—Romans 8:16-17.

There will be a time of great persecution—Luke 21:12.

The wicked despise the godly—Proverbs 29:27.

You will be persecuted—Revelation 2:10.

PRAYER

My Father, it can be frightening to ponder what lies ahead for humanity. Despite the difficult times that are yet to come, however, You have told us not to fear but to rest in Your sovereign oversight of our lives. Please enable us to keep our attention focused on You and not be sidetracked by the distractions of this world. Enable us to remain faithful amid the world's many temptations. Enable us to patiently endure the trials that face us. We also ask that the reality of future judgments motivates us to reach as many people with the gospel as possible. The more people rescued, the better! The more people delivered, the better! In Jesus's name. Amen.

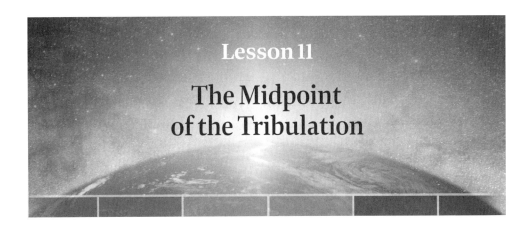

Lesson 11

The Midpoint of the Tribulation

KEY CONCEPT

Conflict will emerge and rise to a fever pitch by the midpoint of the tribulation period. Multiple personalities will be involved in the conflict—the antichrist, the false prophet, Satan, God's two prophetic witnesses, the Jews, and Christians.

THE BIG IDEAS IN THIS LESSON

- The antichrist will be wounded and seemingly resurrect.
- Satan will be cast out of heaven.
- The false religious system affiliated with New Babylon will be destroyed.
- The antichrist will execute God's two prophetic witnesses. God will then resurrect them.
- The antichrist will break his covenant with Israel and desolate the Jewish temple.
- The Jews—now under threat from the antichrist—will escape out of Jerusalem.
- The false prophet will promote the worship of the antichrist, and the antichrist will blaspheme God.
- Satan will make war on Christians.

PROBING THE SCRIPTURES

The Antichrist's Wound and Seeming Resurrection

Read Revelation 13:1-3.

The following page has a mini-commentary:

- "Sea" refers to Gentile nations (Revelation 17:15). The antichrist will be a Gentile.

- The reference to "ten horns and seven heads" reveals that the antichrist will emerge from ten kingdoms, which collectively constitute a revived Roman Empire. The seven heads are the primary rulers of the empire.

- The "ten diadems" refer to the antichrist's extensive dominion.

- The "blasphemous names" point to the antichrist's vile anti-God character.

- The antichrist will be like a leopard (cunning and agile), with feet like a bear's (strong and fierce), and a mouth like a lion's (having a strong bite, or perhaps impressive oratory skills).

There are many views about the "mortal wound" that is healed. Following are two common views:

1. The antichrist will suffer a head wound that is typically fatal, but in this case it is healed by Satan so that the antichrist does not die but lives on. The biblical text tells us that the antichrist "*seemed* to have a mortal wound" (ESV), or "*appeared* to be fatally wounded" (CSB), or it was "*as if* it had been fatally wounded" (NASB). Satan's healing of the wound may give an appearance of resurrection.

2. The second view is that the antichrist will suffer a head wound that will kill him. Satan will then resurrect him from the dead. Against this view is the fact that only God is infinite in power; the devil is finite and limited. Only God can create life (Genesis 1; Deuteronomy 32:39); the devil cannot (Exodus 8:16-19). Only God can raise the dead (John 10:18; Revelation 1:18). Besides, the antichrist will merely *seem to* or *appear to* be killed, so there is no actual need for a resurrection.

My assessment: The antichrist will not actually die or be resurrected. He will be severely wounded and then be healed by Satan. The people of the world will *believe* he has died and been resurrected. They will then worship him because of it.

The antichrist will mimic Christ in many ways during the tribulation period. Summarize what you learn from the following verses:

Deity:

- Christ (John 1:1-2)—

- The antichrist (2 Thessalonians 2:3-4)—

Crowns:

- Christ (Revelation 19:12)—

- The antichrist (Revelation 13:1)—

Kingship:

- Christ (Revelation 19:16)—

- The antichrist (Daniel 11:36)—

Seal/Mark on Followers:

- Christ (Revelation 7:4; 14:1)—

- The antichrist (Revelation 13:16-18)—

Sits on a Throne:

- Christ (Revelation 3:21)—

- The antichrist (Revelation 13:2)—

Armies:

- Christ (Revelation 19:14)—

- The antichrist (Revelation 19:19)—

Given the antichrist's propensity to mimic Christ, do you think it likely he would do almost anything to make the world think he had resurrected from the dead, as Christ did? Explain.

Satan Will Be Cast Out of Heaven

Read Revelation 12:7-13. Satan previously had access to God in heaven. What do we learn about this in Job 1:6-12?

Why do you think Satan will be permanently cast out of heaven at the midpoint of the tribulation?

Explain the contrast between the "woe" and the "rejoicing" at Satan's casting down (12:12).

How "short" is the devil's remaining time?

Does Matthew 8:29 provide us with any insight on evil spirits running out of time?

The False Religious System Will Be Destroyed

The antichrist and the ten kings who are under his authority will now destroy the false religious system affiliated with New Babylon.

Read Revelation 17:15-18. Because the antichrist now seeks to be the sole object of worship on earth, he destroys the false religious system. What do we learn about the antichrist's self-exaltation in the following verses?

- Daniel 11:36-37—

- 2 Thessalonians 2:3-4—

- Revelation 13:5-8—

God's Two Prophetic Witnesses Will Be Executed and Resurrected

God will raise up two prophetic witnesses who will testify to the true God with incredible power during the tribulation period. Their miracles are reminiscent of Elijah (1 Kings 17; Malachi 4:5) and Moses (Exodus 7–11). They will minister during the first half of the tribulation period and will then be martyred by the antichrist.

Read Revelation 11:7-12. Why do you think the bodies of the two prophetic witnesses will be allowed to lie lifeless in Jerusalem for three days?

Why do you think people will exchange gifts at the death of the two prophetic witnesses?

Why will fear erupt when the two prophetic witnesses resurrect from the dead?

The Antichrist Will Break His Covenant with Israel

The antichrist "shall make a strong covenant with many for one week" (Daniel 9:27). This is a "week" of seven years. This means the covenant the antichrist signs with Israel—which allows for temple worship and sacrifices—is designed to remain in effect for a full seven-year period. But the antichrist will double-cross Israel: "For half of the week he shall put an end to sacrifice and offering." The antichrist will renege on the covenant and cause Israel's temple sacrifices to cease.

Here is the chronology:

- The antichrist will relocate to Jerusalem at the midpoint of the tribulation period (Daniel 11:45).

- He will break his covenant with Israel and put an end to temple sacrifices (Daniel 9:27).

- He will set himself up as God (Daniel 11:36-37; 2 Thessalonians 2:4; Revelation 13:7-8).

- He will persecute the Jews (Matthew 24:15-21).

There are two conclusions we can draw:

1. While the antichrist starts out as Israel's *protector*, he now becomes Israel's *persecutor*.

2. While the antichrist starts out as Israel's *defender*, he is now Israel's *defiler*. He defiles the temple by setting up an image of himself within it.

Do you think it is possible that when Satan is ousted from heaven at the midpoint of the tribulation period (Revelation 12:7-9), he will then personally *indwell* the antichrist? Explain.

Details on the Abomination of Desolation

The term "abomination of desolation" conveys a sense of outrage at witnessing a barbaric act of idolatry within God's holy temple (see Daniel 9:27; 11:31; 12:11). Such acts desolate the temple. The abomination of desolation will occur at the midpoint of the tribulation period when the antichrist sets up an image of himself inside the Jewish temple (2 Thessalonians 2:4; Matthew 24:15).

What is the significance of the antichrist setting up an image of himself in the Jewish temple, keeping in mind that Jews view the temple as "the house of the LORD" (1 Kings 6:1)?

Do you think this action of the antichrist might be motivated by Satan? (Satan earlier said, "I will make myself like the Most High"—Isaiah 14:14.)

What insight does 2 Thessalonians 2:9-10 provide on Satan operating through the antichrist?

Since Satan gives the antichrist "his power and his throne and great authority" (Revelation 13:2), might we consider the antichrist to be Satan's puppet during the tribulation period? Explain.

The False Prophet Will Promote Worship of the Antichrist

Read about the false prophet in Revelation 13:11-15.

The false prophet's goal will be to induce people to worship Satan's substitute for Christ—the antichrist (Daniel 9:27; 11:31; 12:11; Matthew 24:15). Toward this end, the false prophet will miraculously animate the image of the antichrist in the Jewish temple so that it seems to be alive (Revelation 13:15).

What do we learn about idols in Psalm 135:15-18?

What do we learn about idols in Habakkuk 2:18-19?

What is the significance of the false prophet giving "breath to the image of the beast, so that the image of the beast might even speak" (Revelation 13:15)? How is this image different from typical idols?

To understand the heinous nature of the false prophet's deception—a deception that leads to the worship of the antichrist—summarize God's command in Exodus 34:14.

The Antichrist Will Blaspheme God

The antichrist "opposes and exalts himself against every so-called god or object of worship, so that he takes his seat in the temple of God, proclaiming himself to be God" (2 Thessalonians 2:4). There is no greater blasphemy than this. The antichrist truly is *anti*-Christ, putting himself in Christ's place.

What do we learn about the antichrist's blasphemy in Revelation 13:5-6?

Given that one's *name* in Bible times represented all that a person is, how will the antichrist's blasphemy against God be especially vile?

Why do you think the antichrist will blaspheme God's "dwelling" and "those who dwell in heaven"?

Jewish Remnant Will Flee from Israel

Read Revelation 12:13-17.

Following is a mini-commentary to help you navigate this passage:

- The "dragon" is a metaphorical reference to Satan, who perpetually stands against Jesus (Matthew 2:13-18; Luke 4:28-30).

- The "woman" is a metaphorical reference to Israel (Isaiah 54:5-6; Jeremiah 3:6-8; 31:31-32; Ezekiel 16:32; Hosea 2:16).

- The "male child" is a reference to Jesus.

- "Two wings of the great eagle" is a metaphorical reference to God's swift deliverance of the Jewish remnant (Exodus 19:4; Deuteronomy 32:11-12).

- "A time, and times, and half a time" refers to a year, two years, and half a year, totaling three-and-a-half years—or half of the tribulation period. God will protect the Jewish remnant in the wilderness for the last half of the tribulation period.

- The phrase, "The serpent poured water like a river out of his mouth," indicates that a satanically driven army will rapidly advance against the Jews like a flood.

- The phrase, "The earth came to the help of the woman," may indicate that the advancing army will be destroyed by a God-induced earthquake that causes the ground to open up and swallow the soldiers (compare with Matthew 24:7; Revelation 6:12; 8:5; 11:13, 19; 16:18).

It is no wonder that Jesus—in His prophetic Olivet Discourse (Matthew 24–25)—points to the need for Jews in Jerusalem to flee for their lives when Satan moves into Jerusalem.

Summarize Jesus's sense of urgency recorded in Matthew 24:15-21.

How does Jeremiah 30:7 describe this difficult time for the Jews?

Satan Will Make War on the Saints

The antichrist will engage in great persecution against both Jews *and* Christians ("saints") during the tribulation period.

How is the antichrist's "war on the saints" (Christians) described in Revelation 13:7-9?

How is the antichrist's "war on the saints" described in Daniel 7:21? (The antichrist is here referred to as a "horn.")

Revelation 13:7 says the antichrist will *conquer* Christians. Daniel 7:21 says the antichrist will *prevail* over them. Why do you think God allows this to happen?

LIFE LESSONS ....

Satan Against Christians

Even now, Satan launches attacks against Christians, seeking to conquer them:

- Satan tempts believers to sin—Ephesians 2:1-3; 1 Thessalonians 3:5.

- Satan tempts believers to lie—Acts 5:3.

- Satan tempts believers to commit sexually immoral acts—1 Corinthians 7:5.

- Satan accuses and slanders believers—Revelation 12:10.

- Satan hinders the work of believers in any way he can—1 Thessalonians 2:17-18.

- Satan and his demons wage war against and try to defeat believers—Ephesians 6:10-12.

- Satan sows tares among believers—Matthew 13:36-43.

- Satan incites persecutions against believers—Revelation 2:10.

- Satan opposes Christians with the ferociousness of a hungry lion—1 Peter 5:8.

- Satan plants doubts in the minds of believers—Genesis 3:1-5.

- Satan seeks to foster spiritual pride in the hearts of Christians—1 Timothy 3:6.

- Satan attempts to lead believers away "from a sincere and pure devotion to Christ"—2 Corinthians 11:3.

Demons Against Christians

- Demons hinder the answers to the prayers of believers—Daniel 10:10-21.

- Demons endeavor to instigate jealousy and faction among believers—James 3:13-16.

- Demons would separate the believer from Christ if they could—Romans 8:38-39.

- Demons cooperate with Satan in working against believers—Matthew 25:41; Ephesians 6:12; Revelation 12:7-12.

DIGGING DEEPER WITH CROSS-REFERENCES

Six Distinct Judgments of Satan

1. Cast from his original position in heaven following his fall—Ezekiel 28:16.
2. Judged in the Garden of Eden—Genesis 3:14-15.

3. Judged at the cross—John 12:31; Colossians 2:15; Hebrews 2:14.

4. Will be cast out of heaven at the midpoint of the tribulation—Revelation 12:7-13.

5. Will be confined to the abyss during the millennial kingdom—Revelation 20:1-3.

6. Will be cast into the lake of fire after the millennial kingdom—Revelation 20:7-10.

The Antichrist's Blasphemy

Blasphemous mouth—Revelation 13:5.

Blasphemous against God and His dwelling place—Revelation 13:6.

Blasphemous names—Revelation 17:3.

Blasphemous nature—2 Thessalonians 2:3-11.

PRAYER

Dear heavenly Father, it is an awesome privilege to come into Your presence. I enter Your gates with thanksgiving, not only for Your many blessings in my life but also for the spiritual armor You provide to protect me against the assaults from wicked spirits.

I put on this armor by faith, beginning with the belt of truth. I am awed that Scripture is "the word of truth" (2 Timothy 2:15) that is inspired by the Holy Spirit, the "Spirit of truth" (John 16:13)—and that Scripture centers on Jesus Christ, "the way, and the truth, and the life" (John 14:6). Thank You, Father, that Your truth anchors my life. Thank You also that Satan cannot stand against Your truth. I ask that Your truth empower me and motivate me this day to live the way You want me to. Please also help me to discern any ways I am being deceived by the wicked one.

By faith, I put on the breastplate of righteousness. Thank You for the imputed righteousness that is mine by faith in Jesus Christ (Romans 3:10-20). I praise You, Jesus, for taking what is mine—my sin—so You could give me what is Yours—Your righteousness (2 Corinthians 5:21). I embrace that righteousness at this moment. I thank You that Satan and his fallen angels must retreat before Your righteousness.

By faith, I put on the shoes of peace, knowing that my peace with You rests entirely on my faith in Jesus, who died for me on the

cross (Romans 5:1). Please also grant me the emotional peace that passes understanding that comes from transferring all my burdens onto Your all-powerful shoulders (Philippians 4:7).

I also take up the shield of faith. May this shield today block all the flaming darts of the evil one—including the soul-crushing darts of depression, discouragement, worry, and guilt. I have faith, Lord, that You are my ultimate shield (Psalm 28:7; 33:20; 119:114; Proverbs 30:5).

By faith, I put on the helmet of salvation. Please protect my mind from intrusive thoughts intended to distract me from following You and trusting You. Please grant that every thought in my mind will be taken captive to obey Christ and His Word (2 Corinthians 10:5). I pray especially that You protect my mind from doubts about You, Your Word, and my relationship with You.

By faith, I take up the sword of the Spirit, which is the Word of God. Today I live in obedience to Your Word (Psalm 119). Today I use the truth of Your Word to defend myself against the lies and deceptions of the devil (Ephesians 6:17). Today I submit my mind for molding by the truths of Your Word. I reject the deceptions of the devil and the evil world system (Romans 12:2).

Father, by faith I have put on the armor. May this be a day of spiritual victory. I bring these petitions before You through the mighty name of our Lord Jesus Christ. Amen.

(This prayer is from my book, *Spiritual Warfare in the End Times,* published by Harvest House.)

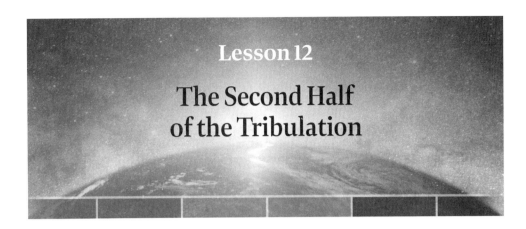

Lesson 12

The Second Half of the Tribulation

▪ KEY CONCEPT

While the phrase "tribulation period" embraces the entire seven years of affliction that will fall upon the world before the second coming of Christ, the last three-and-a-half years constitute the "great tribulation." These will be the most horrific years in human history.

▪ THE BIG IDEAS IN THIS LESSON

- The last three-and-a-half years of the tribulation period constitute the "great tribulation"—especially for Israel.

- During this time, the mark of the beast will be enforced. No one will be able to buy or sell without it.

- Deception will escalate dramatically from Satan, the antichrist, and the false prophet.

- God's most catastrophic judgments—the bowl judgments—will be unleashed upon the world.

- Concurrently, God's grace will continue to shine amid the pervasive darkness. The gospel of the kingdom will be proclaimed throughout the world, bringing many conversions.

▪ PROBING THE SCRIPTURES

The Great Tribulation Will Begin

The events of the second half of the seven-year tribulation period are appropriately called "the great tribulation."

Why are the Gentile nations punished so severely during the great tribulation?

How might Israel's travails during the great tribulation be a necessary prelude to her conversion to Christ at the end of the tribulation? Explain.

Here's the chronology: Once the antichrist puts an end to the animal sacrifices in the Jewish temple, he will desolate the temple by enthroning himself there and then setting up an image of himself within it. This desolation will continue throughout the great tribulation. Once the abomination of desolation has occurred, the Jews living there must immediately escape into the wilderness. Things will soon worsen dramatically. The great tribulation will now be upon them.

Read Matthew 24:15-20. How does Jesus communicate urgency in escaping Jerusalem at this time?

Read Matthew 24:21. What connection is there between the abomination of desolation and the "great tribulation"?

What does Daniel 12:1 say about this time of great tribulation?

What does Jeremiah 30:7 say about this time of great tribulation?

How do Daniel 12:1 and Jeremiah 30:7 communicate the horrific nature of the great tribulation while also showing hope for Israel?

The Mark of the Beast Will Be Enforced

The antichrist and the false prophet—*a satanic diabolical duo*—will subjugate the entire world so that no one can buy or sell who does not receive the mark of the beast.

Read Revelation 13:16-18. Does the false prophet exempt anyone from the mark? Explain.

How would a cashless system of currency make it easy to enforce the mark of the beast? Be specific.

In what ways have cashless systems of currency become increasingly prevalent in recent years?

What do you learn from the following verses about the consequences of receiving the mark of the beast and worshipping the beast or its image?

- Revelation 14:9-11—

- Revelation 16:2—

What does Revelation 20:4 reveal about believers who have refused to receive the mark of the beast?

Summarize how the development of technology intersects with Bible prophecy concerning the mark of the beast.

Human beings in the tribulation period may be branded, just as animals are branded today and as slaves were once branded by slaveholders. We cannot be sure how the number 666 relates to the antichrist or his branding mark. Many theories have been offered. Here are two popular views:

1. Perhaps the number refers to a specific man—a man like the Roman emperor Nero. If Nero's name is translated into the Hebrew language, the numerical value of its letters is 666. Perhaps the antichrist will have the same character as Nero of old.

2. Since the number 7 is a number of perfection, and 777 reflects the perfect Trinity, perhaps 666 points to a being who aspires to perfect deity (like the Trinity) but never attains it. The antichrist, the false prophet, and Satan constitute a diabolical "trinity."

All of this is highly speculative. Scripture does not define what is meant by 666. Even the text of Scripture affirms that understanding what is meant "calls for wisdom" (Revelation 13:18). It may be that the meaning of 666 will not become clear until the antichrist arrives on the world stage in the tribulation period. Those who become believers during this time—and who then attain the wisdom mentioned in Revelation 13:18—may finally understand the significance of the number.

Do you have a view as to the significance of 666? Explain.

Receiving the mark of the beast reveals an implicit approval of the antichrist as a

leader and an agreement with his purpose. No one will take this mark by accident. One must choose to do so, with both eyes open, with all the facts on the table.

There is no middle ground. One chooses either *for* or *against* the antichrist. One chooses either *for* or *against* God.

Historical Insights

- In Bible times, devotees of pagan religions received a tattoo as an emblem of ownership by a particular pagan deity.

- Slaves were branded by their masters. The brand indicated ownership.

- Soldiers were branded by their military leaders. The brand indicated allegiance.

- During the great tribulation, the beast's emblem will somehow be placed on people just as marks were once placed on religious devotees, slaves, and soldiers.

Don't Miss the Connection

Notice that the mark of the beast connects *religion* to the *economy*. These two domains will become merged so that one depends on the other during the great tribulation. The mark of the beast ties them together. This means that even though receiving the mark is essentially a spiritual decision, this spiritual decision will also have life-and-death economic consequences.

> Read James 1:14-15. Summarize the connection between desire, sin, and death.
>
>
> How is James 1:14-15 graphically illustrated with those who choose to receive the mark of the beast?

Deception Will Explode

Deception will explode during the great tribulation.

What role do Satan and the antichrist play in deception (2 Thessalonians 2:9-10)? Why is their deception described as "*wicked* deception"?

How do supernatural signs tie into these wicked deceptions (see Revelation 13:13-14 and 19:20)?

How might the false prophet and the antichrist use deception to induce people to receive the mark of the beast? Can you speculate on what that deception might look like?

Notice that the antichrist engages his work "by the activity of Satan" (2 Thessalonians 2:9). The antichrist is *energized* and *motivated* by Satan.

Bible teacher Ray Stedman once said, "Whom the devil cannot deceive, he tries to destroy, and whom he cannot destroy, he attempts to deceive." Do you think this is true? Why or why not?

What does Jesus say about the character of Satan in John 8:44?

Since Satan energizes the antichrist (2 Thessalonians 2:9), does it make sense to you that the antichrist takes on the lying character of Satan? Explain.

Satan also seeks to tempt Christians to lie and deceive others. What do we learn about this in Acts 5:1-3?

Many unbelievers will turn their backs against God during the tribulation period. God will therefore hand them over to a "strong delusion" (2 Thessalonians 2:11-12). While God does not want any to perish (2 Peter 3:9) and desires all to be saved (1 Timothy 2:3-6), many will refuse God's truth and His offer of salvation. When that happens, God will eventually allow them to experience the full brunt of the consequences of falsehood (Romans 1:18-25). As a form of judgment, God will hand them over to "strong delusion."

Do you have any ideas about what God's "strong delusion" might be? Explain.

What would you say to an atheist who says that a loving God would never hand someone over to "strong delusion"?

God's Bowl Judgments Will Be Unleashed

God will unleash the seal judgments in the first half of the tribulation period, involving bloodshed, famine, death, economic upheaval, a great earthquake, and severe cosmic disturbances (Revelation 6). The trumpet judgments will then be unleashed, involving hail and fire mixed with blood, the sea turning to blood, water turning bitter, further cosmic disturbances, affliction by demonic scorpions, and the death of a third of humankind (Revelation 8:6–9:21).

The worst judgments of all will now fall upon the earth during the great tribulation—*the bowl judgments*. Briefly summarize each judgment:
First bowl judgment (Revelation 16:2)—

Second bowl judgment (Revelation 16:3)—

Third bowl judgment (Revelation 16:4-7)—

Fourth bowl judgment (Revelation 16:8-9)—

Fifth bowl judgment (Revelation 16:10-11)—

Sixth bowl judgment (Revelation 16:12-16)—

Seventh bowl judgment (Revelation 16:17-21)—

(*In the chronology of Revelation, this seventh bowl judgment will occur just after the second coming of Christ. More on this later.*)

The same sun that melts wax also hardens clay. Some people respond to God's judgments with melted hearts and turn to God in repentance and faith. Others harden their hearts against God and refuse to have anything to do with Him. Tragically, many people in the tribulation period will refuse repentance and increasingly harden their hearts against God. They will reject the gospel of the kingdom preached by the 144,000 Jewish witnesses of Christ. Many unbelievers will have fallen prey to the antichrist's deceptive promises and counterfeit miracles.

The Gospel of the Kingdom Will Be Proclaimed

Read Matthew 24:14. Summarize this verse in your own words.

God's light—*His message of redemption*—will continue to shine even in the darkest period of human history. In the "gospel of the kingdom," Jesus will be presented as the divine Messiah/Savior who will reign as King in the coming millennial kingdom and all eternity. Salvation is found only in Him. All who turn to Him in faith will be saved.

> What does it say about God that during the darkest and most rebellious period of human history, He will still give a gracious opportunity for salvation to any who will listen?

Those who turn to the King in faith during the tribulation period will be granted entrance into Christ's thousand-year millennial kingdom. Those who reject the King will be forbidden entrance. At the judgment that takes place following Christ's second coming, Christ will divide all people into goats and sheep (unbelievers and believers). The *sheep* (believers) will be invited into Christ's millennial kingdom. The *goats* (unbelievers) will be sent into punishment (Matthew 25:31-46).

LIFE LESSONS

You Are in a War

While we are not yet in the tribulation period, we are nevertheless in a spiritual war and we are all being targeted by Satan. Here's what you need to know about this war:

- Spiritual warfare is raging all around us (2 Corinthians 10:3-5).

- Spiritual warfare is an integral part of the Christian experience. It is a fact of life. To think a Christian could avoid spiritual warfare is like imagining that a gardener could avoid dealing with weeds.

- In this war, Christians should "wage the good warfare" (1 Timothy 1:18), "fight the good fight of the faith" (1 Timothy 6:12), and be a "good soldier of Christ Jesus" (2 Timothy 2:3).

- You are a targeted person. There's a bull's-eye on your back. You are being stalked and profiled. Your weaknesses and vulnerabilities are being observed and recorded. Satan is locked and loaded, and his bullets have your name on them. *Beware!*

- Not every Christian is at equal risk as a target of Satan. Christians who seek to live for Christ—*those who obey Him and shine His light in a dark world*—are at the highest risk of being attacked by the powers of darkness.

- As a Christian soldier, you must be spiritually prepared for battle. The key to being prepared is to wear God's armor (Ephesians 6:10-18).

- My book, *Spiritual Warfare in the End Times*, may help you. It's published by Harvest House.

Identifying the Antichrist

Many people throughout history have been labeled as the antichrist. Such attempts at identifying the antichrist have always proved to be futile. Past candidates have included:

- Emperor Frederick II
- Napoleon
- Kaiser Wilhelm
- Adolf Hitler
- Joseph Stalin
- Benito Mussolini
- Boris Yeltsin
- Nikita Khrushchev
- John F. Kennedy (targeted by anti-Catholics)
- Henry Kissinger
- Margaret Thatcher
- Mikhail Gorbachev
- Ronald Wilson Reagan (he had six letters in each of his three names)
- Bill Clinton (Hillary was claimed to be the false prophet)
- Prince William

Here's the lesson we learn: We should avoid attempting to guess the identity of the antichrist. If you're a Christian, you will be raptured out of the world before his manifestation (2 Thessalonians 2:1-3). If you're around to recognize the antichrist, then you've probably been left behind.

Deception in the End Times

Many will not endure sound teaching—2 Timothy 4:3-4.

Many will succumb to the doctrines of demons—1 Timothy 4:1.

Widespread apostasy will occur—2 Thessalonians 2:3.

Mark of the Beast

Contrasts with the seal of the living God—Revelation 7:2-4.

The false prophet will force it on people—Revelation 13:16.

No one can buy or sell without it—Revelation 13:17.

The alternatives are persecution or death—Revelation 13:7, 10, 15, 17.

It invokes God's fury—Revelation 14:9-10.

Gospel of the Kingdom

Will be proclaimed throughout the whole world—Matthew 24:14.

Will be declared by 144,000 Jewish converts—Revelation 7 and 14.

The result will be a "great multitude" of believers—Revelation 7:9-10.

PRAYER ·

> *Father, as I continue to study biblical prophecy, I ask that You daily*
> *transform my life into what You want it to be. Romans 13:12-13*
> *tells us, "The day is at hand. So then let us cast off the works of*
> *darkness and put on the armor of light. Let us walk properly as in*
> *the daytime." By Your grace, please enable me to cast off the works of*
> *darkness and walk in the light. I pray in the name of Jesus. Amen.*

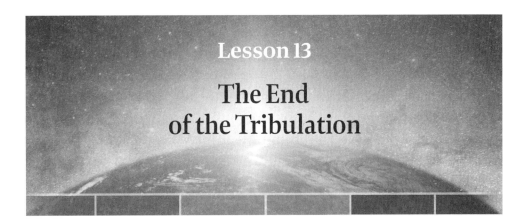

Lesson 13

The End of the Tribulation

▩ KEY CONCEPT

The campaign of Armageddon will explode on the scene at the end of the tribulation period. Millions of people will perish in the worst escalation of conflict ever to hit planet Earth. The climax will be Christ's second coming and the defeat of the antichrist and his forces.

▩ THE BIG IDEAS IN THIS LESSON

- The allied armies of the antichrist will gather for the final destruction of the Jews.

- New Babylon will be destroyed and will become desolate. The entire world will grieve at the sight of New Babylon's demise.

- Jerusalem will fall and be ravaged by the antichrist's forces.

- The antichrist and his forces will then move south to attack the Jewish remnant.

- The Jewish remnant—now endangered—will experience national regeneration and call upon their Messiah (Jesus) for deliverance.

- Jesus will return in glory to rescue the Jewish remnant.

- The final battle will erupt. Christ will effortlessly annihilate the antichrist and his vast forces.

- Christ will victoriously ascend to the Mount of Olives.

▩ PROBING THE SCRIPTURES

The Campaign of Armageddon Will Begin

Earth's population will have already been traumatized from the ever-worsening seal judgments, trumpet judgments, and bowl judgments. Worse comes to worst when the catastrophic war campaign called Armageddon erupts upon the earth (Daniel 11:40-45; Joel 3:9-17; Zechariah 14:1-3; Revelation 16:12-16). This takes place at the very end of the tribulation period. Millions of people will perish in the worst escalation of conflict ever to hit planet Earth.

The term *Armageddon* literally means "Mount of Megiddo." It refers to a location about sixty miles north of Jerusalem. This is where Barak battled the Canaanites (Judges 4) and Gideon battled the Midianites (Judges 7). This will be the site for the final horrific battles of humankind just before the second coming of Christ.

Notice that Armageddon involves *battles*. Some people erroneously refer to "the battle of Armageddon," as if it is a single conflict that is over in a relatively short time. Contrary to this misconception, Armageddon will involve an extended, escalating conflict, and it will be catastrophic.

In what follows, we will explore the various stages in the unfolding campaign of Armageddon.

The Antichrist's Allies Will Assemble for War

The allied armies of the antichrist will gather for the ultimate destruction of the Jews.

> Read Revelation 16:12-16. What is the source of the demonic spirits?
>
>
>
> How do you think these wicked spirits will go about gathering world leaders for Armageddon? How will they use signs (seemingly miraculous acts) to accomplish their goal?

The goal of this gathered coalition will be to once and for all destroy the Jewish people. Each member of the satanic trinity—Satan, the antichrist, and the false prophet—will be involved. Demons, too, will participate.

> Can you think of other ways Satan has sought the destruction of the Jews throughout biblical history?

New Babylon Will Be Destroyed

A revived Babylon—what we might call New Babylon—will be rebuilt by the antichrist and will be dominant during the tribulation period (Revelation 17–18). During the first half of the tribulation period, it will be the headquarters of a global religious system that influences the entire world. During the second half of the tribulation period (the great tribulation), it will function as the economic and political center of the world.

The antichrist will start his rise to power in a revived Roman Empire. He will soon come into global dominion. At the midpoint of the tribulation period, he will set up headquarters in Jerusalem. At this time, he will claim to be God and will set up an image of himself in the Jewish temple. In the latter part of the tribulation period, the antichrist will shift his headquarters to New Babylon, which will become a global commercial center. This commercial center will likely control the oil fields—and the money these fields generate—in the Middle East. It will be destroyed during Armageddon.

What do we learn about New Babylon's destruction in the following Bible passages?

- Jeremiah 50:13-14—

- Jeremiah 50:23-25—

- Jeremiah 50:39-40—

- Isaiah 13:19-22—

- Revelation 18:21-24—

Who are the attackers of the antichrist's New Babylon?

- Jeremiah 50:9—

- Jeremiah 50:41-46—

Notice two things:

1. Just as Babylon was used in Old Testament times as God's rod of discipline against Israel, God will now use a northern coalition as His whipping rod against Babylon.

2. Just as Babylon showed no mercy in its oppression of Israel, so God will now show no mercy to Babylon.

Summarize James 2:13 in your own words.

Jerusalem Will Fall and Be Ravaged

The destruction of the antichrist's capital—New Babylon—will not be enough to distract him from his overarching goal of destroying the Jewish people. Instead of launching a counterattack against the northern military coalition that wiped out New Babylon, the antichrist and his forces press on in attacking Jerusalem.

What do we learn about this attack from the following Bible passages?

- Zechariah 12:1-3—

- Zechariah 14:1-3—

- Since "all the nations" will be gathered against Jerusalem, do you think the United States will be included in this group? Explain.

- Do you think the United States will become an ally of the antichrist during the tribulation period?

Jerusalem will fall and be ravaged in the face of this overwhelming international attack force. However, the Messiah will soon come to the rescue of the Jewish remnant in the wilderness.

The Antichrist's Forces Will Move South Against the Jewish Remnant

Not all the Jews will be in Jerusalem when the antichrist and his forces attack. Many Jews will have previously escaped Jerusalem when the antichrist desolates the Jewish temple at the midpoint of the tribulation period (see Matthew 24:15-31). The remnant will now likely be in the vicinity of Bozrah/Petra, about eighty miles south of Jerusalem.

How is the Jewish great escape from Jerusalem described in the following verses (keep in mind that the "woman" refers to Israel or the Jews):

- Revelation 12:5-6—

- Revelation 12:13-14—

This remnant of Jews—south of Jerusalem—will now become the antichrist's target. These Jews will sense impending doom as the forces of the antichrist gather in the rugged wilderness, poised to attack and eradicate them. They will be helpless. From an earthly perspective, they will be utterly defenseless.

The Endangered Jewish Remnant Will Experience National Regeneration

The Jewish remnant will be endangered. They will be acutely aware that the antichrist's forces have gathered to destroy them. Hope is not lost, however. At this juncture, God will remove their spiritual blindness, and they will finally recognize Jesus as their divine Messiah. The remnant will experience national regeneration. They will become born again.

A quick review of Jewish history helps us understand this better.

Read Romans 11:25. What does the apostle Paul say about God's discipline of the Jews for rejecting Jesus as the Messiah?

Why does God turn His attention away from the Jews and toward Gentile salvation?

The Jews botched it. Instead of seeking a faith-relationship with God through Jesus Christ, they had sought to do everything the law prescribed so they could *earn* a relationship with God.

What do we learn about this from Romans 9:30-33?

What does Galatians 2:15-16 tell us about the impossibility of salvation by good works?

Failure for the Jews was unavoidable. Attaining righteousness by observing the law requires it to be kept *perfectly* (James 2:10), which no human being can do. The Jews refused to admit their inability to keep the law perfectly. To make matters worse, they rejected Jesus as the Messiah, refusing to turn to Him in faith because He did not fit their preconceived ideas about the Messiah (Matthew 12:14, 24).

Because of Israel's stubbornness, God inflicted a partial blindness or hardness of heart upon the Jews as a judgment. Israel thus lost her favored position before God, and the gospel was preached to the Gentiles to cause the Jews to become jealous and then become saved (Romans 11:11). Israel's hardening and casting off was always intended to be temporary.

Now, at Armageddon the armies of the antichrist will be gathered in the desert wilderness, poised to attack the Jewish remnant. At this desperate point, God—in His perfect timing—will remove the blindness from their eyes. They will promptly repent and turn to their divine Messiah, Jesus Christ, for deliverance.

> How does Hosea 6:1-3 describe this national repentance and belief in the divine Messiah?

In dire threat at Armageddon, Israel will plead for their newly found Messiah to return and deliver them (Zechariah 12:10; Matthew 23:37-39). This He will do without delay.

Jesus Will Return in Glory

The prayers of the Jewish remnant will be quickly answered! The divine Messiah will return personally to rescue the Jewish remnant from danger.

> What do you learn about the second coming from the following verses?
>
> • Revelation 19:11-16—
>
>
> • Revelation 1:7—

- Matthew 24:29–31—

- Luke 21:25-28—

- Acts 1:10-11—

- Colossians 3:4—

- Hebrews 9:27-28—

- Jude 14-15—

- Revelation 22:12-13—

Five titles are used of Jesus as related to His second coming. What are they, and what is their significance (Revelation 19:11-21)?

- Title 1—

- Title 2—

- Title 3—

- Title 4—

- Title 5—

If you knew the precise time of Christ's second coming, would that change the way you live? Explain.

The Final Battle Will Erupt and Christ Will Destroy the Antichrist's Forces

At His second coming, Jesus will confront the antichrist and his forces and slay them with the word of His mouth. Instant deliverance will come to the Jewish remnant.

What do you learn from the following verses about Christ's defeat of the antichrist?

- Habakkuk 3:13—

- 2 Thessalonians 2:8—

The antichrist will be impotent in the face of the true Christ. The antichrist's forces will be destroyed, from Bozrah all the way back to Jerusalem.

What do we learn about this in Joel 3:12-13?

What do we learn about this in Revelation 14:17-20?

Christ Will Victoriously Ascend the Mount of Olives

Following the defeat of the antichrist and his forces, Jesus will victoriously ascend the Mount of Olives.

How is this described in Zechariah 14:3-4?

At this juncture, we learn of Christ's final judgment before the tribulation period ends. Christ unleashes the horrific seventh bowl judgment.

How is this final judgment on the earth described in Revelation 16:17-21?

When Christ ascends to the Mount of Olives, cataclysmic events will be unleashed that bring an end to the tribulation period:

- An earthquake of globally staggering proportions will occur.
- Jerusalem will be split into three areas.
- The Mount of Olives will be split into two parts, creating a valley.
- There will be a horrific hailstorm.

As these events subside, the tribulation period ends.

LIFE LESSONS •

Be Patient

Some mockers say, "Where is the promise of his coming? For ever since the fathers fell asleep, all things are continuing as they were from the beginning of creation" (2 Peter 3:4). God has a reason for the delay, for He "desires all people to be saved and to come to the knowledge of the truth" (1 Timothy 2:4). "The Lord is not slow to fulfill his promise as some count slowness, but is patient toward you, not wishing that any should perish, but that all should reach repentance" (2 Peter 3:9).

The Blessings of the Second Coming

It's easy to lose sight of the great significance of the blessings of the second coming for believers. Here are two of the more noteworthy:

1. Christ will set up His kingdom of perfect righteousness on earth.

2. You and I, as resurrected believers, will be with Christ not only during the millennial kingdom but throughout all eternity. We ought to live daily with great anticipation.

DIGGING DEEPER WITH CROSS-REFERENCES

The Second Coming

It will be a glorious appearing—Titus 2:11-14.
Christ will be on a white horse—Revelation 19:11.
Christ will come in great power and glory—Matthew 24:30.
It will be accompanied by cosmic phenomena—Matthew 24:29.
The sign of the Son of Man will appear in the heavens—Matthew 24:30.
Every eye will see Him—Revelation 1:7.
Christ will be followed by the armies of heaven—Revelation 19:14.

Readiness for the Second Coming

Await the Master—Luke 12:36.
Be on alert, for we don't know when the Master is coming—Mark 13:35-37.
Be ready—Matthew 25:10-12; Luke 12:35.
Be sober-minded—1 Thessalonians 5:6; 1 Timothy 3:2, 11; Titus 1:8; 2:2, 12; 1 Peter 1:13; 4:7.
He will come when we don't expect it—Matthew 24:44.

Father, I thank You for the clear teaching of Your Word that the church will be raptured before the tribulation period. You have told us that You have not "destined us for wrath" (1 Thessalonians 5:9). That means we won't suffer through the wrath that will fall at Armageddon. Your Word teaches us that at the height of Armageddon, raptured believers will be among Your armies who return with You at the second coming (Revelation 19:14). How wondrous it is to ponder such things. I praise You for the salvation I have in Jesus Christ. It is in His name that I pray. Amen.

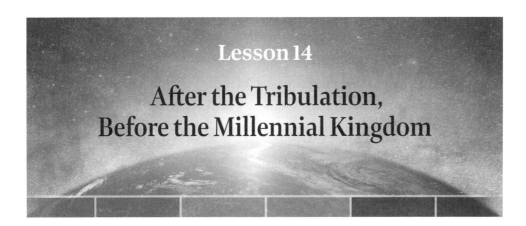

Lesson 14

After the Tribulation, Before the Millennial Kingdom

KEY CONCEPT

There will be seventy-five days between the end of the tribulation and the beginning of the millennial kingdom. This interim period will bring closure to the tribulation and allow time for preparations for the coming kingdom.

THE BIG IDEAS IN THIS LESSON

- Christ will judge the Gentile nations at the beginning of the seventy-five-day period. He will separate the "sheep" (believers) from the "goats" (unbelievers) and invite the sheep into the kingdom. The goats will be sent into fiery punishment.

- Christ will also judge the Jews who survive the tribulation period. Jews who have trusted in Jesus the Messiah for salvation (the believing remnant) will be invited into the kingdom. Unbelieving Jews will suffer the same fate as unbelieving Gentiles—fiery punishment.

- Jesus (the divine Bridegroom) and the church (His bride) will enjoy a marriage feast. It will be an unforgettably joyous occasion.

- Final preparations will be made for the beginning of the millennial kingdom.

PROBING THE SCRIPTURES

A 75-Day Transitional Interim Begins

A calculation of days in prophetic Scripture reveals a seventy-five-day interim between the end of the tribulation period and the beginning of the millennial kingdom. On the following page is how we arrive at the number:

- Daniel 12:12 speaks of the second half of the tribulation period and beyond: "Blessed is he who waits and arrives at the 1,335 days."

- We already know that the second half of the tribulation period is 1260 days, which is precisely three-and-a-half years (Revelation 11:3).

- Here is some simple math: 1335 minus 1260 equals 75.

- Since the millennial kingdom has not yet begun, this can only mean there is a seventy-five-day time span between the end of the tribulation period and the beginning of the millennial kingdom.

- Further examination of prophetic Scripture reveals that several key events take place during this interim period.

The Nations Will Be Judged

Read Matthew 25:31-46.

This passage describes the judgment of the nations, which will immediately follow the second coming of Christ after the tribulation period. Believers and unbelievers from among the nations are pictured as sheep and goats. They are portrayed as being intermingled and require separation by a special judgment. As a result of this judgment, believers (the sheep) will enter Christ's thousand-year millennial kingdom while unbelievers (the goats) will depart into fiery punishment.

Christ will judge the Gentiles according to how they treated His "brothers" during the tribulation period. In Christ's reckoning, treating His brothers kindly is the same as treating Him kindly. Treating His brothers with contempt is the same as treating Him with contempt.

Why does Christ speak this way about the close connection between Him and His followers? Be specific.

How do we see this same close connection between Himself and His followers in the following passages?

- Acts 9:1-5—

- Matthew 10:40—

- Luke 10:16—

- 1 Corinthians 6:17—

- 1 Corinthians 8:10-13—

- Ephesians 5:29-30—

- 1 John 5:20—

How will Christ commend the righteous (Matthew 25:35-36)?

How will Christ condemn the unrighteous (Matthew 25:42-43)?

A comparison of this passage with the details of the tribulation suggests that the "brothers" are the 144,000 Jewish evangelists mentioned in Revelation 7 and 14. These are Christ's *Jewish* brothers who faithfully bear witness of Him during the tribulation.

Even though the antichrist and the false prophet will wield control over the world during the tribulation period (Revelation 13), God will still be at work. God's

redeemed—the sheep—will come to the aid of Christ's Jewish brethren with food and water (and meet other needs) as these Jewish evangelists bear witness to Christ all around the world.

Read James 2:14-17. How do the sheep—in caring for Christ's brothers—illustrate James's point?

Based on what you've learned about Christ's brothers and the truths in James 2:14-17, formulate a one-sentence principle about how Christians ought always to be open to helping brothers and sisters in Christ.

Formulate another one-sentence principle about how Christians today ought always to be open to materially supporting those involved in Christian ministry, such as pastors and ministers whose work is similar to that of the brothers.

What insights can you derive from the following passages on supporting those in Christian ministry?

- Philippians 4:15-19—

- 1 Thessalonians 5:12-13—

- 1 Timothy 5:17-18—

Here is an interesting fact: When the "sheep" enter Christ's millennial kingdom, they will do so in their mortal bodies and continue to get married and have babies

throughout the millennium. Their bodies will *not yet* be transformed into glorified eternal bodies. This means that even though longevity will characterize the millennial kingdom, both mortal Jews and Gentiles who enter the kingdom will continue to age and die (Isaiah 65:20-25). They will be resurrected following the millennial kingdom (see 1 Corinthians 15:50-55).

The Jews Will Be Judged

Read Ezekiel 20:33-38.

Christ will not only judge the Gentiles during the seventy-five-day interim period, He will also judge the Jews during this time. Jews from all over the world will be gathered together for this judgment. Christ will purge out all the rebels—all those who have refused to turn to Him for salvation.

Read John 5:22-23. Why did the Father assign all judgment to Jesus, the Son?

What do we learn about Jesus the Judge in Acts 10:42?

What do we learn about Jesus the Judge in James 5:9?

What do we learn about Jesus the Judge in Revelation 19:11?

Believers among the gathered Jews will be invited to enter Christ's millennial kingdom. This is the faithful remnant. Once in the kingdom, they will experience a full possession of the Promised Land (Genesis 12:1-3; 15:18-21; 17:21; 35:9-12) and the reestablishment of the Davidic throne (2 Samuel 7:5-17), upon which Christ will rule. God will fulfill all the land and crown promises He made to Israel in Old Testament times. God is a promise keeper!

While Christ's reign on David's throne is yet future (in the millennial king-dom), does Christ *presently* have a free reign on the throne of your heart? Explain.

What do we learn about God as a promise keeper in the following verses?

- Numbers 23:19—

- Joshua 21:45—

- Joshua 23:14—

- 1 Kings 8:56—

- Hebrews 10:23—

What does it mean to you personally that God is a promise keeper? Explain.

The Divine Bridegroom and His Bride Will Enjoy a Marriage Feast

Previously we noted that Scripture describes the relationship between Christ and the church using a marriage motif, with Christ being the Bridegroom and the church being the bride of Christ (Matthew 9:15; 22:1-14; 25:1-13; Mark 2:18-20; Luke 5:33-35; 14:15-24; John 3:29). To understand the full significance of the marriage feast that is celebrated during the seventy-five-day interim period, it is helpful to review the three phases in Hebrew weddings:

1. The bride became betrothed to the bridegroom.

2. The bridegroom came to claim his bride after preparing a place to live in his father's house.

3. The groom, bride, and family celebrated a marriage supper—a feast lasting several days, even up to a week.

We see these three phases in Christ's relationship to the church:

1. As individuals living during the church age come to salvation, they become a part of the church, the bride of Christ, betrothed to the divine Bridegroom.

2. The Bridegroom (Jesus Christ) will come to claim His bride at the rapture. At this time, He will take the bride to heaven—the Father's house—where He has prepared a place to live (John 14:1-3). The actual marriage will take place in heaven following the rapture.

3. The marriage feast of the Lamb will take place on earth during the seventy-five-day interval between the end of the tribulation period and the beginning of the millennial kingdom. It will be an incredible spectacle.

How does the marriage motif emphasize the incredibly close and intimate relationship between Christ and His people? Be specific.

A famous song about heaven is titled "I Can Only Imagine." Try to imagine what the marriage feast between Christ and the church might be like. Jot down any thoughts or reflections here:

Final Preparations for the Millennial Kingdom

Final preparations for the beginning of the millennial kingdom will also likely transpire during the seventy-five-day interim period:

1. The antichrist and the false prophet will no longer be permitted to attack God's people. They will be cast alive into the lake of fire (Revelation 19:20).

2. Satan will be bound in the bottomless pit for a thousand years (Revelation 20:1-3).

3. Christ will set up the governmental structure of the millennial kingdom (2 Timothy 2:12; Revelation 20:4-6). Faithful Christians will reign with Christ, and Christ will likely hand out governmental assignments at this time.

4. Tribulation saints who were martyred by the antichrist will be resurrected from the dead. They, too, will participate in reigning with Christ for a thousand years (Revelation 20:4).

What have you learned in this chapter that strengthens your faith in God?

What have you learned in this chapter that excites you about what is to come?

What have you learned in this chapter about how you ought to live as a Christian during your remaining years on earth?

LIFE LESSONS ·

Faithful While Waiting

In biblical times, a betrothed woman would eagerly await the coming of her groom to take her away to his father's house (see John 14:1-3). During this time of anticipation, the bride's fidelity to her groom was tested. Likewise, as the bride of Christ (the church) awaits the coming of the messianic Groom, the church is called to live in purity and godliness until He arrives at the rapture.

What do you learn about this call to purity from the following passages?

- Romans 13:11-14—

- 2 Peter 3:10-14—

- 1 John 3:1-3—

Is your lifestyle befitting a bride who is awaiting the soon appearance of her Bridegroom? Are there any changes you need to make in your life?

Enduring Trials and Tribulations

God calls His people to patiently endure amid trials and tribulations. We're not in the tribulation period yet, but we all have our share of trials and tribulations. Contrary to what we might intuitively think, these trials can be beneficial to us.

- The book of James emphasizes: "Count it all joy, my brothers, when you meet trials of various kinds, for you know that the testing of your faith produces steadfastness. And let steadfastness have its full effect, that you may be perfect and complete, lacking in nothing" (James 1:2-4).

- James also urges: "Blessed is the man who remains steadfast under trial, for when he has stood the test he will receive the crown of life, which God has promised to those who love him" (James 1:12).

- First Peter 1:6-7 tells us: "In this you rejoice, though now for a little while, if necessary, you have been grieved by various trials, so that the tested genuineness of your faith—more precious than gold that perishes though it is tested by fire—may be found to result in praise and glory and honor at the revelation of Jesus Christ."

Be encouraged. Patiently endure through your trials and tribulations. God will grow your faith through them.

DIGGING DEEPER WITH CROSS-REFERENCES

The Bridegroom and His Bride

The church now awaits her Bridegroom—2 Corinthians 11:2.

Jesus is preparing a place to live for His bride—John 14:1-3.

The marriage and marriage supper of the Lamb is yet future—Revelation 19:6-9.

Metaphors of the Church

The bride of Christ—Revelation 21:1-2.

A "new man"—Ephesians 2:14-16.

The body of Christ—Colossians 1:18.

One body with many members—Romans 12:4-5; 1 Corinthians 12:12.

God's temple—1 Corinthians 3:16-17.

God's household—Ephesians 2:19-20; 1 Timothy 3:14-15.

A spiritual house—1 Peter 2:4-5.

Jesus as a Judge

The great Judge is coming—James 5:9.

He is Judge of all—Acts 10:42.

We must all stand before Christ—2 Corinthians 5:10.

Our deepest secrets will be exposed—Romans 2:15-16; 1 Corinthians 4:5.

He will judge the world—Acts 17:30-31.

Father, as I consider the many details of Your prophetic plan for the future, I've come across so many verses that cause me to rejoice in Your control of all things. You have asserted, "My counsel shall stand, and I will accomplish all my purpose" (Isaiah 46:10). You affirm: "As I have planned, so shall it be, and as I have purposed, so shall it stand" (Isaiah 14:24). You are "the blessed and only Sovereign, the King of kings and Lord of lords" (1 Timothy 6:15). "Many are the plans in the mind of a man, but it is the purpose of the Lord that will stand" (Proverbs 19:21). "No wisdom, no understanding, no counsel can avail against the Lord" (Proverbs 21:30). You are awesome, Lord. You are worthy to be praised. Your glory and majesty are wondrous things to ponder. I pray and rejoice in Jesus's name. Amen.

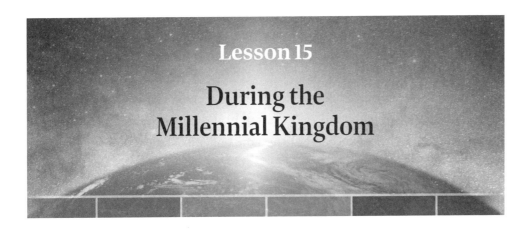

Lesson 15

During the Millennial Kingdom

■ KEY CONCEPT

Following Christ's establishment of the millennial kingdom, all living believers—both Jews and Gentiles—will be invited to enter. The kingdom will be characterized by a perfect government, physical blessings, and spiritual blessings.

■ THE BIG IDEAS IN THIS LESSON

- Christ will set up the millennial kingdom.

- Following the judgment of the nations and the judgment of the Jews, Gentile and Jewish believers will be invited to enter the kingdom.

- Israel will be fully restored and take full possession of the Promised Land.

- A millennial temple will be built. It will be the heart and center of millennial worship.

- Christ will reign over the millennial earth from the Davidic throne in Jerusalem.

- Christians who were raptured prior to the tribulation period will participate in reigning with Christ.

- Christ will bring about incredible physical blessings on the millennial earth.

- Christ's government will be perfect in every way.

- Christ will pour out incredible spiritual blessings on the millennial earth.

■ PROBING THE SCRIPTURES

The Millennial Kingdom Will Begin

Jesus will set up His thousand-year kingdom on earth following His second coming. In theological circles, this is known as the millennial kingdom. *Millennium* comes from two Latin words—*mille*, which means "thousand," and *annum*, which means "year."

In the chronology of the book of Revelation, the millennial kingdom will follow the second coming of Jesus Christ. Revelation 19 and 20 are chronological, with the second coming described in chapter 19 and the millennial kingdom in chapter 20.

Read Isaiah 9:6. What five titles are used of Jesus as related to the millennial kingdom, and what is their significance?

What do you learn about the nature of the millennial kingdom from the following Bible passages?

- Isaiah 65:17-23—

- Jeremiah 31:10-14—

- Ezekiel 34:25-31—

- Joel 2:21-27—

- Amos 9:13-15—

- Micah 4:1-5—

Tribulation Believers Will Enter the Millennial Kingdom

Gentiles will face Christ at the judgment of the nations, which follows Christ's second coming (Matthew 25:31-46). Those found to be believers will be invited into Christ's millennial kingdom in their mortal bodies (25:34, 46).

The Jews will face Christ at a separate judgment. The redeemed remnant among the Jews will be invited to enter the kingdom in their mortal bodies (Ezekiel 20:33-38).

People will live much longer during the millennial kingdom. Nevertheless, both mortal Jews and Gentiles will continue to age and die (Isaiah 65:20). Married couples among both groups will continue to have children throughout the millennium. All who die during this time will be resurrected at the end of the millennium.

Some children of the believers who enter the kingdom will not become believers. After a few years have passed, some who are born during the early days of the millennium will grow to adulthood rejecting the Savior-King in their hearts—though outwardly obeying His government. The same will be true of some grandchildren, great-grandchildren, and the like. Some of these unbelievers will eventually participate in the final revolt against God at the end of the millennium, under Satan's lead. (Satan will be released from the Abyss after the thousand years—Revelation 20:7-10.)

Why do you think some people who witness the incredible spiritual and physical blessings of Christ's millennial kingdom will still refuse to believe in Him for salvation?

What does it say about Christ that He allows unbelievers to continue living in His millennial kingdom?

Though 1 Timothy 2:3-4 does not relate specifically to the millennial kingdom, do you think this verse might nevertheless reveal the Lord's heart in allowing unbelievers to continue living in His kingdom?

Though 2 Peter 3:9 does not relate specifically to the millennial kingdom, do you think this verse might nevertheless reveal the Lord's heart in allowing unbelievers to continue living in His kingdom?

Israel Will Be Restored and Possess the Land

Read Jeremiah 31:31-34. Summarize in one sentence how the new covenant promises the regeneration of Israel.

The new covenant promises the necessary internal power for the Jews to obey God's commands—something the Mosaic covenant of the law could never accomplish. The new covenant promises a complete national regeneration of Israel, and every Jew who enters the millennial kingdom will personally know the Lord.

Israel will not only experience regeneration in fulfillment of the new covenant, but will also be fully regathered in their land. The land covenant in Deuteronomy 29–30 is eternal and unconditional. God promised that even though Israel would be dispersed worldwide, the Jews would be regathered and restored to the land. This restoration will take place in Christ's millennial kingdom.

What do we learn in Isaiah 43:5-7 about this regathering of the Jews?

This regathering to the Promised Land is highly significant from a prophetic standpoint. It all relates to God's land promises to Abraham a long time ago.

Read Genesis 15:18-21. How are the land boundaries of the Promised Land specified?

How did God reaffirm the land promises to Abraham's son Isaac (Genesis 26:1-5)?

How did God reaffirm the land promises to Isaac's son Jacob (Genesis 28:10-15)?

Summarize Psalm 105:7-11 in your own words.

After God regathers the Jews from around the world, they will finally come into *full possession* of the land that God promised them. This fulfillment will come thousands of years after the promise was initially given. But God is utterly faithful. God promised it long ago, and now He will fulfill the promise at the beginning of Christ's millennial kingdom.

A Millennial Temple Will Be Built

A millennial temple will be built (Ezekiel 40–48), and animal sacrifices will be instituted (Isaiah 56:6-7; 60:7; Jeremiah 33:17-18; Zechariah 14:19-21). This millennial temple will be the final temple for Israel. Its dimensions make it significantly larger than any other temple in Israel's history.

Why do you think it necessary that this will be the largest temple ever?

This massive temple will facilitate God's presence among His people during the millennium (Ezekiel 37:26-28). God's presence (and His glory) will enter the temple, and He will be with them. This temple will also be a worship center of Jesus during the millennium. (Jesus, of course, is God, just as the Father is.)

The temple will be constructed at the beginning of the messianic kingdom (Ezekiel 37:26-28) by Christ (Zechariah 6:12-13), by redeemed Jews (Ezekiel 43:10-11), and even by representatives from the Gentile nations (Zechariah 6:15; Haggai 2:7). All will join together in its construction.

> What is the unifying factor of these Jews and Gentiles? What do they have in common?
>
>
>
>
> How will this temple benefit both Jewish and Gentile believers?

Many wonder why animal sacrifices will be restored in the millennial kingdom. The purpose of the sacrifices is to remove ceremonial uncleanness from the temple itself—that is, to prevent defilement from polluting the purity of the temple environment. Such ceremonial cleansing will be necessary because Yahweh (our holy God) will again be dwelling on the earth amid sinful—and therefore unclean—mortal people.

Remember, these believers survive the tribulation period and enter the millennial kingdom in their mortal bodies—*still in full possession of their sin natures*, even though redeemed by Christ. The sacrifices will thus remove any ceremonial uncleanness in the temple.

Seen in this light, the sacrifices are most certainly not a return to the Mosaic law. The law is forever antiquated in Jesus (Romans 6:14-15; 7:1-6; 1 Corinthians 9:19-21; 2 Corinthians 3:7-11; Galatians 4:1-7; 5:18; Hebrews 8:13; 10:1-14). The sacrifices relate *only* to removing ritual impurities in the temple, as fallen-though-redeemed human beings remain on earth.

> Try to imagine what it will be like to witness God's incredible glory filling this immense temple. Jot down any thoughts or reflections here.
>
>
>
>
> Do you think people in the millennium might respond to God's glory in the temple as the ancient Jews did in 2 Chronicles 7:1-3? Explain.

Christ Will Reign from the Davidic Throne

God made a covenant with David in which He promised that one of his descendants would rule forever on the throne of David (2 Samuel 7:12-13; 22:51). This is an unconditional covenant. It did not depend on David's merit (or any lack of merit) for its fulfillment.

This covenant finds its ultimate fulfillment in Jesus, who was born from the line of David (Matthew 1:1). Prophetic Scripture often affirms that Christ will rule from the throne of David during the millennial kingdom.

What do you learn about Christ's future dominion from the following messianic prophecies?

- Psalm 72:8—

- Isaiah 9:6-7—

- Daniel 7:13-14—

Resurrected Saints Will Reign with Christ

While Christ will gloriously reign from the Davidic throne, raptured (resurrected) faithful believers will be privileged to reign with Christ.

What do you learn about this from the following Bible verses?

- 2 Timothy 2:12—

- Revelation 5:9-10—

- Revelation 20:6—

- Revelation 22:5—

The particular role of each Christian in reigning with Christ will be commensurate with their commitment and faithfulness during earthly life.

How do Jesus's words in Matthew 25:14-30 illustrate this?

Reigning with Christ	
Believers are a *kingdom of priests* and will reign with Christ.	Revelation 5:9-10; 20:6
If we endure, we will reign with Christ.	2 Timothy 2:12
Christ's *martyrs* will reign with Him.	Revelation 20:4
Overcoming Christians will sit on the throne with Christ.	Revelation 3:21
Christ's *servants* will reign forever.	Revelation 22:5

Christ Will Bring Many Physical Blessings

Those who enter Christ's millennial kingdom will enjoy some rather unique physical blessings. Consult the following verses and summarize what you learn from each.

People will live in a blessed and enhanced environment:

- Isaiah 35:1-2—

There will be plenty of rain for the ground and hence plenty of food for animals:

- Isaiah 30:23-24—

- Isaiah 35:5-7—

Animals will live in harmony with each other and with humans, their predatory and carnivorous natures having been removed:

- Isaiah 11:6-7—

Longevity will be significantly increased:

- Isaiah 65:20—

Physical infirmities and illnesses will be removed:

- Isaiah 29:18—

- Isaiah 33:24—

Prosperity will prevail, resulting in joy and gladness:

- Jeremiah 31:12-14—

Christ Will Institute a Perfect Government

Christ will institute a perfect government in the millennial kingdom. Consult the following verses and summarize what you learn.

Christ's government will be global:

- Psalm 2:6-9—

- Daniel 7:14—

The global government will be centered in Jerusalem:

- Isaiah 2:1-3—

- Jeremiah 3:17—

- Ezekiel 48:30-35—

- Zechariah 8:1-3—

Jesus will reign on the throne of David:

- Jeremiah 23:5-6—

Christ's government will be perfect and effective:

- Isaiah 9:6-7—

Christ's government will bring lasting global peace:

- Micah 4:3-4—

Christ Will Bestow Great Spiritual Blessings

Christ will bring great spiritual blessings to His millennial kingdom. These blessings relate to Christ Himself being present with His people on earth.

Isaiah the prophet tells us that "the earth shall be full of the knowledge of the LORD as the waters cover the sea" (Isaiah 11:9). Meanwhile, Satan and demons will be bound during the millennial kingdom (Revelation 20:1-3).

The spiritual blessings that will predominate during the millennial kingdom are based on the new covenant (Jeremiah 31:31-34). Consult the following verses and summarize what you learn:

The Holy Spirit will be present and will indwell all believers:

- Ezekiel 36:27—

- Ezekiel 37:14—

- Isaiah 32:15—

- Isaiah 44:3—

- Joel 2:28-29—

Righteousness will prevail around the world:

- Isaiah 46:12-13—

- Isaiah 51:5—

- Isaiah 60:21—

Obedience to the Lord will prevail:

- Psalm 22:27—

- Jeremiah 31:33—

Holiness will prevail:

- Isaiah 35:8-10—

- Joel 3:17—

Faithfulness shall prevail:

- Psalm 85:10-11—

- Zechariah 8:3—

There will be unified worship of the Messiah by the world's residents:

- Malachi 1:11—

- Zephaniah 3:9—

- Zechariah 8:23—

God's presence will be made manifest:

- Ezekiel 37:27-28—

- Zechariah 2:10-13—

LIFE LESSONS

Worshipping God

Worship will be a central feature of Christ's millennial kingdom (Ezekiel 43–46). Worship should also be a central feature of our lives. Psalm 95:6-7 instructs:

> Oh come, let us worship and bow down;
>> let us kneel before the LORD, our Maker!
> For he is our God,
>> and we are the people of his pasture,
>> and the sheep of his hand.

Worship involves reverencing God, adoring Him, and praising Him, not just outwardly in a corporate setting but in our hearts as well.

Christ Is King

Genesis 49:10 prophesied that the Messiah would come from Judah's tribe and reign as king. The Davidic covenant promised a Messiah who would have an eternal throne (2 Samuel 7:16; Luke 1:32-33). Psalm 110 affirms that the Messiah will rule over all. In Revelation 19:16, Jesus comes again as the "King of kings and Lord of lords."

I've asked the question previously, but it bears repeating: *Is Christ presently enthroned in your heart?*

DIGGING DEEPER WITH CROSS-REFERENCES

Millennial Kingdom

Follows the second coming—Isaiah 66.

Christ's earthly thousand-year reign—Revelation 20:1-3.

The glorious reign of Christ—Isaiah 52:7-12.

The Lord will reign and judge people righteously—Psalm 96.

Jesus will rule on the throne of David—Isaiah 9:6-7; Jeremiah 23:5-6; 33:17-26.

Christ supreme in all the earth—Psalm 68:32-35; 110:1-3; Isaiah 2:1-2; 52:10.

Christ will restore Israel—Isaiah 25:7-8; 30:26; 51:11-16; 65:17-19.

Israel to rejoice in blessings of restoration—Isaiah 35; Zephaniah 3:14-20.

Blessings of the millennial kingdom—Isaiah 35.

There will be universal peace and blessing—Psalm 46:8-9; Isaiah 2:4; 9:5-7; 11:6-9.

Millennial blessings will extend to the Gentiles—Isaiah 56:1-8.

Earth will be filled with knowledge of the Lord—Habakkuk 2:14.

There will be peace—Isaiah 19:24-25.

There will be great productivity—Isaiah 35.

Christ will crush wickedness—Isaiah 2:2-4, 9-21; 24:1-23.

There will be a millennial temple in Jerusalem—Ezekiel 40–48.

Satan will be bound during the millennial kingdom—Revelation 20:1-3.
Satan will be loosed at the end of the millennium to deceive the nations—Revelation 20:7-10.

PRAYER ·····································

Father, as I ponder the reality that Christ is King, it causes me to examine my life for areas where I may not be living in complete submission to my King. Search my heart, O God, and show me areas of my life that call for unconditional surrender. Help me to understand that the abundant life Jesus promised hinges on a life that is fully surrendered to Him as my sovereign King. May it be so! I pray in Jesus's name. Amen.

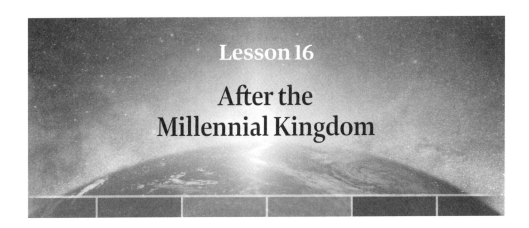

Lesson 16

After the Millennial Kingdom

■ KEY CONCEPT

Satan will be released from the Abyss after the millennial kingdom and will lead one final revolt against God and His people. God will quickly bring judgment upon Satan and the rebels who join him. Satan will be cast into the lake of fire. The wicked dead will then be resurrected, judged, and cast into the lake of fire.

■ THE BIG IDEAS IN THIS LESSON

- Satan will be released from the Abyss after the millennial kingdom and lead one final revolt against God. By that time, there will be many unbelievers on earth, and many of these will join Satan in this revolt. God will bring instant judgment on the rebels by sending down fire from heaven.

- Satan will be cast into the lake of fire, where the antichrist and false prophet are already burning. This satanic trinity will suffer there for all eternity.

- The "second resurrection"—the resurrection of the wicked dead—will then occur. (The "first resurrection" is the resurrection of believers.)

- The wicked dead will face Christ at the great white throne judgment. They will not only be condemned but will also be assigned varying degrees of punishment.

- Following the great white throne judgment, the wicked dead will be cast into the lake of fire where they will suffer for eternity.

■ PROBING THE SCRIPTURES

Satan Will Lead a Final Revolt

Satan will be quarantined in the bottomless pit—*the Abyss*—during Christ's thousand-year millennial kingdom. This quarantine will effectively remove a powerful and destructive force from those who live during Christ's millennial kingdom.

Read Revelation 20:1-3. What angel do you think is powerful enough to throw Satan into the bottomless pit?

Read Revelation 20:7-10. Why do you think God allows Satan to be released from the Abyss so he can attempt to deceive the nations?

What insight does John 8:44 provide on Satan as a deceiver?

How is it possible that people "as numberless as sand along the seashore" (Revelation 20:8 NLT) will join Satan after living in a perfect world governed by Christ Himself for so long?

Here's my take on this last question: Only redeemed Jews and Gentiles will initially enter the millennial kingdom in their mortal bodies—*still possessing a sinful nature*. Some of their children, grandchildren, great-grandchildren (and so forth) *will not* become believers (though many will). By the time a thousand years have passed, there will be many unbelievers on earth who will succumb to their sinful natures and join Satan in this last rebellion.

Jerusalem will be the target city of this satanic revolt. Jerusalem will be the headquarters of Christ's government throughout the millennial kingdom (Isaiah 2:1-5).

Read Revelation 20:9. Describe God's judgment on the invaders in your own words.

Fire is a common mode of God's judgment in Bible times. What do you learn about this from the following verses?

- Genesis 19:24-25—

- Exodus 9:23-24—

- Leviticus 10:1-3—

- Numbers 11:1-3—

- 2 Kings 1:9-14—

Satan Will Be Cast into the Lake of Fire

Read Revelation 20:10.

All three persons of the satanic trinity—Satan, the antichrist, and the false prophet—will suffer the same fiery fate. The antichrist and the false prophet will be thrown into the lake of fire before the beginning of the millennial kingdom. They will have been burning there for a thousand years when Satan will join them—and all three will continue to burn for all eternity.

Many today wonder how eternal punishment in the lake of fire can be reconciled with the love of God. What do you think?

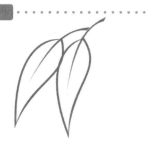

We learn elsewhere that Satan is not the only fallen angel who will be judged and confined to the lake of fire. All demons who have served under him will also be judged and consigned there.

> What insights do we gain on this from Matthew 25:41?
>
>
> What insight does 2 Peter 2:4 provide?
>
>
>
> How do you think our lives will qualitatively change with Satan and demons out of the picture forever and ever?

The Second Resurrection Will Then Take Place

The "second resurrection" will take place in preparation for the great white throne judgment—the judgment of the wicked dead.

> Read John 5:25-29. What did Jesus say about different resurrections?

The first and second resurrections are *types* of resurrection (see Revelation 20:5-6, 11-15). The first resurrection is the resurrection of Christians. God's people are resurrected at different times—some at the rapture, some after the tribulation period, and some at the end of the millennial kingdom. All of these are part of the first resurrection.

God's people will now have bodies in which the perishable has become imperishable and the mortal has become immortal (1 Corinthians 15:53-55). These bodies will be specially designed to enable us to live directly in the presence of God for all eternity. These bodies will perpetually be sick-free and death-free.

The second resurrection is sobering. It is the resurrection of the wicked dead in preparation for facing Christ at the great white throne judgment (Revelation 20:13). Regardless of what century they lived in, the unsaved dead of all time will be resurrected to face Christ. Their bodies will be *indestructible* resurrection bodies and capable of experiencing pain in the lake of fire forever and ever.

How does God's judgment relate to His attributes of holiness and justice?

Is the reality of the lake of fire a motivation for you to engage in evangelism?

Do you have a family member or friend whose eternal destiny is questionable? Is there anything you can do about it?

The Wicked Dead Will Be Judged

The great white throne judgment takes place *after* the millennial kingdom, for Revelation 20—after describing the millennium—states: "*Then* I saw a great white throne and him who was seated on it" (verse 11). In other words, the millennium takes place first, and *then* the judgment takes place.

This judgment will not separate believers from unbelievers, for all who will experience it will have already chosen during their lifetimes to reject God. Once they are before the divine Judge, they are judged according to their works not only to justify their condemnation but to determine the degree to which each person should be punished throughout eternity.

When Christ opens the book of life, no name of anyone present at the great white throne judgment is in it. Their names do not appear in the book of life because they have rejected the *source* of life—Jesus Christ.

Read Revelation 20:12. What is the book of life?

What insights about the book of life do you gain from the following Bible passages?

- Psalm 69:28—

- Hebrews 12:22-23—

- Revelation 3:5—

- Revelation 13:7-8—

- Revelation 17:8—

- Exodus 32:30-34—

- Philippians 4:3—

As a Christian, how does it make you feel that your name was written in God's book of life before the world was even created? Does it give you a sense of security?

The other books mentioned in Revelation 20:12 detail the lives of the unsaved. They will supply the evidence to substantiate the divine verdict of a destiny in the lake of fire.

What do the following Bible passages reveal about how the lives of unbelievers will be evaluated at the judgment?

- Actions (Psalm 62:11-12; Ecclesiastes 12:14; Matthew 16:27)—

- Words (Matthew 12:36-37)—

- Thoughts and motives (Jeremiah 11:20; Luke 8:17; 1 Corinthians 4:5; Revelation 2:23)—

Scripture indicates that there will be degrees of punishment experienced in the lake of fire.

What insights do we glean from the following passages about degrees of punishment?

- Matthew 10:15—

- Matthew 16:27—

- Luke 12:47-48—

- Revelation 22:12—

Common observation shows that unsaved people vary as much in their quality of life as saved people do. Some saved people are spiritual while others are carnal. Some unbelievers are terribly evil (like Hitler), while others seek to live more virtuously.

Just as believers differ in how they respond to God's law, and hence in their reward in heaven, so unbelievers differ in their response to God's law, and hence will have corresponding punishment in the lake of fire. Just as there will be degrees of reward in heaven, so there will be degrees of punishment in the lake of fire. *God is perfectly just in assessing human beings.*

God's Judgment	
After death comes judgment	Hebrews 9:27
Believers judged by Christ	1 Corinthians 3:10-15; 2 Corinthians 5:10
Day of judgment coming	2 Peter 3:7
Every deed judged	Ecclesiastes 12:14
Unbelievers judged at great white throne judgment	Revelation 20:12
Inevitable	Jeremiah 44:15-28
Judgment awaits all	Matthew 12:36-37; Romans 14:10-12
Motivates holiness	2 Corinthians 5:9-10; 2 Peter 3:11-14
Motivates repentance	Acts 17:30-31
Nations judged at the second coming	Joel 3:2; Matthew 25:31-46
Nothing kept secret from God	Hebrews 4:13

The Lake of Fire Will Be Populated

Satan, the antichrist, the false prophet, and unbelievers of all ages will find their eternal home in the lake of fire (Revelation 19:20; 20:10-15). All residents will be tormented day and night forever and ever.

The lake of fire—also called "hell"—is a real place. But it was not part of God's original creation, which He called "good" (Genesis 1). Hell was later created to accommodate the banishment of Satan and his fallen angels who rebelled against God (Matthew 25:41). Human beings who reject Christ will join Satan and his fallen angels in this infernal place of suffering.

This infernal place of suffering is known by many terms and is described in many ways in Scripture. What insights do we gain from the following verses?

- Matthew 13:41-42—

- Revelation 19:20—

- Matthew 18:8-9—

- Matthew 25:46—

- Matthew 7:13—

- 2 Thessalonians 1:5-9—

Bible expositors love to debate the "fire" of hell. Some believe it is literal. Others say it is a metaphorical way of expressing the great wrath of God.

What do you learn about fire as an expression of God's wrath in the following verses?

- Deuteronomy 4:24—

- Hebrews 12:28-29—

- Nahum 1:6—

- Malachi 3:1-2—

- Jeremiah 4:3-4—

What is your personal view? Does the lake of fire involve literal fire, or is fire an expression of God's wrath?

Do you think it is possible that the term *fire* might be both literal *and* an expression of God's wrath? How so? (Full disclosure: This view seems logical to me.)

Any way you look at it, it will be awful!

LIFE LESSONS

Fear of Judgment Can Lead to Conversions

Fear of a future judgment and the possibility of a destiny in the lake of fire have moved many to become Christians throughout the centuries. J.C. Ryle, an Anglican bishop who lived from 1816 to 1900, said: "People will never set their faces decidedly towards heaven, and live like pilgrims, until they really feel that they are in danger of hell." This was one of the components of the Great Awakening in the English colonies in America during the 1730s and 1740s. Fear of an eternity in hell sparked large-scale revival.

Are you moved to personal revival in view of the fact that you will face Christ at the judgment seat of Christ?

Time Is Running Out

None of us can pinpoint the moment of our deaths. The great evangelist George Whitefield, who lived from 1714 to 1770, said: "How do you know, O man, but the next step you take may be into Hell? Death may seize you, judgment find you, and then the great gulf will be fixed between you and endless glory forever and ever." Perhaps this is why the apostle Paul said, "Now is the day of salvation" (2 Corinthians 6:2). Don't wait until it's too late. If you are not a believer, secure your salvation today by faith in Jesus Christ, the wonderful Savior (John 3:16; 6:40; 11:25-26).

DIGGING DEEPER WITH CROSS-REFERENCES

The Binding of Satan

Satan will be bound in the bottomless pit during the millennium—Revelation 20:1-3.

The bottomless pit is a place of imprisonment for demons—Luke 8:30-31; 2 Peter 2:4.

Satan will be released at the end of the millennium to deceive the nations—Revelation 20:7-9.

Satan will be finally judged and cast into the lake of fire—Revelation 20:10.

The Lake of Fire

Beast and false prophet thrown in—Revelation 19:20.

Death and Hades thrown in—Revelation 20:14.

Devil thrown in—Revelation 20:10.

Sinners thrown in—Revelation 21:8.

Those not in the book of life thrown in—Revelation 20:15.

Eternal fire—Matthew 18:8; Mark 9:47-48.

Fiery furnace—Matthew 13:41-42.

Fiery lake of burning sulfur—Revelation 19:20; 21:8.

God's wrath poured out like fire—Nahum 1:6; Deuteronomy 4:24; Jeremiah 4:3-4; Malachi 3:1-2.

Eternal punishment—Matthew 25:46; 2 Thessalonians 1:5-9.

Gloomy dungeons—2 Peter 2:4.

Not part of God's original creation—Matthew 25:41.

Torment—Luke 16:19-24.

Weeping and gnashing of teeth—Matthew 13:41-42.

PRAYER

Father, when I consider the destiny of the wicked, it makes me all the more appreciative of my salvation in Jesus Christ, for I know I do not merit salvation in myself. I can do nothing to deserve eternal life with You in heaven. I am ever aware of my sins. If not for Your grace and mercy, openly displayed in Jesus dying for me on the cross, I too would be lost. I take this moment to praise You for what You've done for me. Thank You for my salvation. Thank You for eternal life. I pray in Jesus's name. Amen.

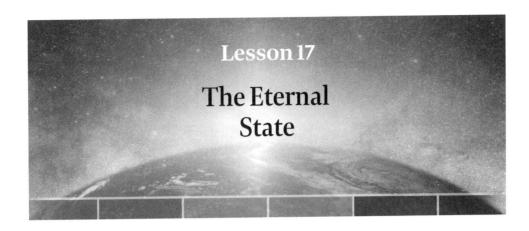

Lesson 17
The Eternal State

▨ KEY CONCEPT

God will create a new heaven and a new earth. Upon the new earth will rest the New Jerusalem—the eternal city where Christians will live with God forever.

▨ THE BIG IDEAS IN THIS LESSON

- God will destroy the old heavens and the old earth. All vestiges of sin and Satan will be removed.

- God will then create a new heaven and a new earth, which will be specially suited for the eternal state.

- The New Jerusalem—the eternal city where we will dwell for all eternity—will rest upon the new earth. Christ Himself is the architect and builder of the New Jerusalem.

- We will live face to face with God. There will be no more sin, Satan, death, sorrow, or mourning. All will be perfect.

▨ PROBING THE SCRIPTURES

The Old Heavens and the Old Earth Will Be Destroyed

God placed a curse on the earth following Adam and Eve's sin against God (Genesis 3:17-18). Romans 8:20 affirms that "all creation was subjected to God's curse" (NLT). Redeemed humans cannot live eternally in a cursed creation. This is why the earth—along with the first and second heavens (the earth's atmosphere and the stellar universe)—will be dissolved by fire. The old order will be dissolved to make way for a new heaven and a new earth.

What do we learn about the temporal nature of the present earth and the first and second heavens in the following verses?

- Psalm 102:25-26—

- Matthew 24:35—

Satan has long carried out his evil schemes on earth (Ephesians 2:2). The stains resulting from his extended presence must therefore be purged. Satan will have no place in the new heaven and the new earth. God will remove all evidence of his influence when He dissolves the earth and the heavens. What is stained and decaying must make room for what will be pure and eternal.

What do we learn about the dissolving of the present heavens and earth in the following verses?

- 2 Peter 3:7—

- 2 Peter 3:10—

What does 2 Peter 3:11-13 say about how we should live as Christians in view of all this?

God Will Create a New Heaven and a New Earth

Though the present universe will be destroyed, God will create a new heaven and a new earth for us to dwell in forever. All things will be made new, and how blessed it will be!

The Greek word used to designate the newness of the cosmos is *kainos*, which means "new in nature" or "new in quality." Hence, the phrase "a new heaven and a new earth" refers not to a cosmos that is totally other than the present cosmos. Rather, the new cosmos will stand in continuity with the present cosmos, but it will be completely renewed and renovated. It will be gloriously rejuvenated. It will be perfectly transformed. We might say that resurrected believers will live on a resurrected earth in a resurrected universe!

What do you learn about the newness of heaven and earth from Revelation 21:1-5?

What insights can you glean from Isaiah 65:17?

An incredible thing to ponder is that one day heaven and earth will no longer be separate realms, as they are now, but will be merged. Believers will thus continue to be in heaven even while they are on the new earth. The new earth will be utterly sinless, bathed and suffused in the light and splendor of God, unobscured by evil of any kind or tarnished by evildoers.

The New Jerusalem Will Rest Upon the New Earth

The New Jerusalem—the heavenly city—will be our eternal residence. The description of the New Jerusalem in Revelation is astounding. We witness such transcendent splendor that the human mind can scarcely take it in. This is a scene of ecstatic joy and fellowship of sinless angels and redeemed, glorified human beings. The voice of the One identified as the Alpha and the Omega—the beginning and the end—utters a climactic declaration: "Look, I am making everything new" (Revelation 21:5 NLT).

The words of Revelation 21 and 22 represent a human attempt to describe the indescribable. As wonderful as John's description is, the reality will likely far exceed what mere words can convey. The city will be unimaginably splendorous. The beauty will be incomprehensible.

Read Revelation 21–22. What emotions run through you upon reading this description? Be specific.

How do you think the description of the New Jerusalem compares with the description of the Garden of Eden (Genesis 2:8-15)?

Why do you think angels are posted at each of the twelve gates of the New Jerusalem?

Why do you think the names of the twelve tribes of Israel are inscribed on the gates?

Why do you think the names of the apostles appear on the foundations of the city?

What do you think is the significance of the river of the water of life?

What do you think is the significance of the restoration of the tree of life to human beings in the afterlife?

The New Jerusalem will reflect the incredible glory of God. The mention of transparent gold reveals that the city will transmit the glory of God in the form of light without hindrance. Human imagination is incapable of fathoming the resplendent glory of God that will perpetually be on display in the eternal city. This is especially so when we consider that the eternal city is brimming with countless precious stones.

What do you learn from the following verses about God's (and Jesus's) resplendently glorious light—powerful enough to illuminate a large city?

- James 1:17—

- 1 John 1:5—

- 1 Timothy 6:13-16—

- Matthew 17:1-2—

- Revelation 1:16—

The New Jerusalem will be a literal city, a real place where real resurrected people and a holy God will dwell together. A city has dwellings, bustling activity, various kinds of gatherings, and much more. There is no warrant for taking the descriptions of the New Jerusalem in Scripture as merely symbolic. Every description we have of the New Jerusalem in the Bible implies a real place of residence—albeit a resplendently glorious residence.

The heavenly city measures about 1500 miles by 1500 miles by 1500 miles. It is so huge that it would measure approximately the distance from Canada to Mexico, and from the Atlantic Ocean to the Rockies. It has a surface area of 2.25 million square miles.

The city is tall enough that it would reach about one-twentieth of the way to the moon from the earth's surface. If the city has stories, each being twelve feet high, then the city would have 600,000 stories. *That is huge!*

> Read Revelation 21:1-2. How is it possible that you and I—*fallen sinners*—can live forever in "the holy city"?
>
>
>
> Who makes us holy (Hebrews 10:10, 14; 13:12)?

You and I need not personally attain moral perfection to live in the eternal city. Those of us who believe in Christ have been given the very righteousness of Christ (Romans 4:11, 22-24). Because of Jesus, we have been made holy (Hebrews 10:14). Hence, we will have the privilege of living in the holy city for all eternity.

Notice the contrasts between earthly cities and the New Jerusalem:

- Earthly cities must constantly be rebuilt or repaired, but no such repair is ever necessary in the New Jerusalem.

- Believers and unbelievers live in earthly cities, but only believers will be in the eternal city.

- Many people go hungry and thirsty in earthly cities, but no one will hunger or thirst in the New Jerusalem.

- Earthly cities have crime, but there is perfect righteousness in the eternal city.

- Earthly cities often have outbreaks of rebellion, but there is no such rebellion in the heavenly city. All are in submission to the divine King, Jesus Christ.

- People in earthly cities have many broken relationships, but all relationships in the New Jerusalem are perfect and loving.

- Widespread disease is common in earthly cities, but perfect health predominates in the New Jerusalem.

- Earthly cities have graveyards, but such are absent in the eternal city. (Death will entirely be foreign to our experience in heaven.)

- Earthly cities get dark at night, but the eternal city is always lighted.

Finally, the purposes of God are fulfilled. God's plan of salvation—conceived in eternity past—is now brought into full fruition. How glorious it will be!

Pondering our eternal future vitalizes our inner being. It can give us strength to face the hardships of life.

What do we learn about pondering heaven in Colossians 3:1-4?

Make an honest assessment of your life. Do you think you live more like a citizen of earth or a citizen of heaven?

Do you make a habit of keeping a top-down perspective—a *heavenly* perspective? How might this practice help you to face earthly problems and difficult circumstances with a greater sense of spiritual peace?

Think about some of your Christian loved ones who are now in heaven. Does your future reunion with them put wind in your spiritual sails?

LIFE LESSONS . . . .

God Will Dwell Among Us

In the Garden of Eden, God walked among Adam and Eve (Genesis 1–3). Once sin entered the world, God dwelt among the Israelites via the Jewish tabernacle (Exodus 40:34) and later the temple (2 Samuel 22:7). In New Testament times, God "tabernacled" among us in the person of Jesus (John 1:14). Today, Christians are the temple of the Holy Spirit (1 Corinthians 3:16; 6:19-20). In the New Jerusalem, God will personally dwell with His people *face-to-face* (Revelation 22:4).

Your Citizenship

Even though we live in different cities on earth, we are ultimately citizens of heaven. The apostle Paul said, "Our citizenship is in heaven, and from it we await a Savior, the Lord Jesus Christ" (Philippians 3:20). Paul also said that we are "fellow citizens with the saints and members of the household of God" (Ephesians 2:19). We are pilgrims passing through on earth, on our way to another country, another land, another city (Hebrews 11:16).

Here is something you must not forget: We are to behave here *below* as citizens of that city *above*.

Jonathan Edwards's Resolutions

Jonathan Edwards suggests the following spiritual resolutions:

- "Resolved, to endeavor to obtain for myself as much happiness, in the other world, as I possibly can."

- "Resolved, that I will live so as I shall wish I had done when I come to die."

- "Resolved, to endeavor to my utmost to act as I can think I should do if I had already seen the happiness of heaven and hell's torments."

Would you like to adopt Edwards's resolutions as your own? Explain.

Would you like to make any other resolutions? List them here.

DIGGING DEEPER WITH CROSS-REFERENCES

Eternity

Eternal life is promised from the beginning of time—Titus 1:1-3.
Election is from all eternity—Ephesians 1:3-4; 2 Timothy 1:8-9.
God is eternal—Isaiah 44:6; 57:15.
We will have eternal resurrection bodies—2 Corinthians 5:1-10.

Jesus is eternal—Revelation 1:17-18.

God inhabits eternity—Isaiah 57:15.

God put eternity in the human heart—Ecclesiastes 3:11.

God has an eternal purpose—Ephesians 3:11-12; 2 Timothy 1:8-10.

Jesus is from eternity past—Micah 5:2.

Eternal State

All things will be new—Revelation 21:5.

Creation eagerly awaits redemption—Romans 8:19-21.

Eternal glory awaits us—2 Corinthians 4:17-18.

In the Father's house are many rooms—John 14:1-3.

An eternal inheritance awaits us—1 Peter 1:3-5.

There will be a new heaven and a new earth—Revelation 21:1-4.

There will be no more curse, no more night—Revelation 22:3-5.

Our resurrection bodies live forever—2 Corinthians 5:1.

We will shine—Daniel 12:3.

Some Final Reflections

Take a few moments to ponder these final reflections:

1. "Time is short. Eternity is long. It is only reasonable that this short life be lived in the light of eternity." (*Charles Spurgeon*)

2. "We do well to think of the long tomorrow." (*A. W. Tozer*)

3. "The best is yet to be." (*John Wesley*)

4. "A heavenly mind is a joyful mind." (*Richard Baxter*)

5. "It ought to be the business of every day to prepare for our last day." (*Matthew Henry*)

6. "Eternity is primary. Heaven must become our first and ultimate point of reference. We are built for it, redeemed for it, and on our way to it. Success demands that we see and respond to *now* in the light of *then*." (*Joseph Stowell*)

7. "If you read history you will find that the Christians who did most for the present world were precisely those who thought most of the next." (*C.S. Lewis*)

8. "Let's not get too settled in, too satisfied with the good things down here on earth. They are only the tinkling sounds of the orchestra warming up.

The real song is about to break into a heavenly symphony, and its prelude is only a few moments away." (*Joni Eareckson Tada*)

My Father, I fear that the attractions of this world sometimes sidetrack me so that I live more like a citizen of this world than a citizen of heaven. Please enable me, by Your grace, to take my heavenly citizenship more seriously. How I yearn to be with You in the New Jerusalem, dwelling face-to-face with You for all eternity. I long for the day when there will be no more tears, mourning, or death. All of this is made possible because of the salvation Jesus attained for me at the cross. How thankful I am for Jesus! It is in His name that I pray. Amen.

Final Thoughts

Our journey through prophetic Scripture has come to a close. We've touched on prophecies in many Bible books, from Genesis to Revelation. I want to close our time together by showing you how the books of Genesis and Revelation are bookends. What began in Genesis comes to fruition in Revelation. The promises made in Genesis find final fulfillment in Revelation. Things that went wrong for humankind in Genesis are redeemed and restored in Revelation. It is amazing to ponder it all.

Please allow your mind to feast upon the following inspirational truths:

- In the beginning, God created the heavens and the earth (Genesis 1:1). In the eternal state, a new heaven and a new earth await us (Revelation 21:1-2).

- In the beginning, the sun and moon were created as "two great lights" (Genesis 1:16-18). The eternal state entails an eternal city where there is no longer any need for such light, for the glory of God lights up the eternal city of the redeemed (Revelation 21:23; 22:5).

- In the beginning, God created the night (Genesis 1:5). The eternal state involves a nightless eternity (Revelation 22:5).

- In the beginning, God created the seas (Genesis 1:10). The new earth in the eternal state will no longer have a sea (Revelation 21:1).

- In the beginning, human beings succumbed to Satan's temptations (Genesis 3:1-7). In the eternal state, Satan will be perpetually quarantined from the people of God (Revelation 20:10).

- In the beginning, God pronounced a curse following humankind's fall into sin (Genesis 3:16-19). In the eternal state, there will be no more sin and no more curse (Revelation 22:3).

- In the beginning, paradise was lost (Genesis 3:22-24). In the eternal state, paradise will be gloriously restored for redeemed humans (Revelation 2:7).

- In the beginning, Adam and Eve were barred from the tree of life (Genesis 3:22-24). In the eternal state, redeemed humans will enjoy restoration to the tree of life (Revelation 2:7; 22:2, 14, 19).

- In the beginning, tears, death, and mourning entered human existence (Genesis 2:16-17; 37:34-35). In the eternal state, tears, death, and mourning will be forever absent from the redeemed (Revelation 21:4).

- In the beginning, a Redeemer was promised (Genesis 3:15). In the eternal state, the victorious Redeemer reigns (Revelation 20:1-6; 21:22-27; 22:3-5).

The great news is that we can experience *all* of this because of what Jesus has done for us in salvation. We can't earn it. We can't be "good enough" to warrant it. We can't make ourselves worthy of it. But each of us—fallen sinners every one—can participate in this grand reversal because of the salvation we have in Jesus (Ephesians 2:8-9). *Never forget what Jesus Christ has done for us:*

- We are *saved* in Christ (Hebrews 7:25).

- We are *forgiven* in Christ (Ephesians 1:6-7).

- We are *justified* in Christ (1 Corinthians 6:11).

- We are *reconciled* in Christ (Colossians 1:19-20).

- We are *redeemed* in Christ (Ephesians 1:7).

- We are *made alive* in Christ (Romans 6:11).

- We are *brought near* in Christ (Ephesians 2:11-13).

- We have *eternal life* in Christ (Romans 5:20-21).

How great a *Redeemer* we have in Christ!
How great a *salvation* we have in Christ!
How great an *eternal future* we have in Christ!

WE CAN ONLY EXULT:
To him who loves us
and has freed us from our sins by his blood
and made us a kingdom,
priests to his God and Father,
to him be glory and dominion forever and ever.
Amen
(Revelation 1:5-6).

No One Knows the Day or the Hour...
But You Can Know the Order of Events

You've heard of the rapture, the great tribulation, the mark of the beast, and other prophetic topics, but do you know how they fit together? This chronological tour through all of the Bible's most important predictions of end-time events reveals...

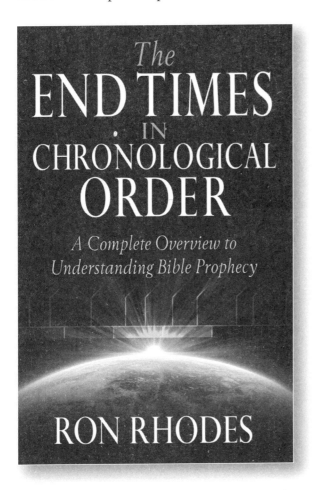

- when important end-time events will happen in relation to each other

- who the major players in the end-time drama will be

- how to interpret the signs of the times

- how Old Testament and New Testament prophecies fit together

- why you can trust a literal interpretation of the Scriptures

God intends for you to understand His Word—including end-time prophecies. The more you learn, the more you will come to love and trust the Scriptures and the God who inspired them.

Other Great Harvest House Books
by Ron Rhodes

Basic Bible Prophecy

40 Days Through Genesis

The Big Book of Bible Answers

Commonly Misunderstood Bible Verses

Find It Fast in the Bible

The Popular Dictionary of Bible Prophecy

Understanding the Bible from A to Z

8 Great Debates of Bible Prophecy

40 Days Through Daniel

40 Days Through Revelation

Cyber Meltdown

New Babylon Rising

End Times Super Trends

Jesus and the End Times

The End Times in Chronological Order

Northern Storm Rising

Unmasking the Antichrist

Spiritual Warfare in the End Times

Israel on High Alert

Secret Life of Angels

What Happens After Life?

Why Do Bad Things Happen If God Is Good?

Wonder of Heaven

Reasoning from the Scriptures with the Jehovah's Witnesses

Reasoning from the Scriptures with Mormons

Coming Oil Storm (eBook only)

Topical Handbook of Bible Prophecy (eBook only)

To learn more about our Harvest Prophecy resources, please visit:

www.HarvestProphecyHQ.com

HARVEST PROPHECY
AN IMPRINT OF HARVEST HOUSE PUBLISHERS

YOU CAN UNDERSTAND BIBLE PROPHECY FOR YOURSELF

In today's tumultuous world, we see current events aligning with what will happen during the tribulation period prophesied in the Bible. The uncertainty of what is to come has led many to ask questions about what will happen, and when.

With this companion to *The End Times in Chronological Order*, author Ron Rhodes provides a strategically designed guide to help you unpack Bible prophecy. Whether you journey through this workbook on its own or in tandem with the book, this resource illuminates every key concept believers need to know—and where they fit on God's timeline—from the rapture to the tribulation and the return of Christ, and beyond.

Let your heart be enriched, nurtured, and emboldened as you experience the blessing the book of Revelation promises to those who study Bible prophecy! *The End Times in Chronological Order Workbook* will equip you to better understand and prepare for what God has made known about the future.

RON RHODES, (ThD), president of Reasoning from the Scriptures Ministries, is heard regularly on nationwide radio and is the author of *Basic Bible Prophecy*, *The 8 Great Debates of Bible Prophecy*, and *40 Days Through Revelation*. He periodically teaches at Dallas Theological Seminary and several other seminaries.

AN IMPRINT OF
HARVEST HOUSE PUBLISHERS

Prophecy / Bible Study Guides
ISBN 978-0-7369-8538-3

51799

9 780736 985383   U.S. $17.99